Chef
in Your
Backpack

Gourmet Cooking in
the Great Outdoors

Nicole Bassett

P9-BZM-659

ARSENAL PULP PRESS

VANCOUVER

CHEF IN YOUR BACKPACK
Copyright © 2003 by Nicole Bassett

ARSENAL PULP PRESS
103-1014 Homer Street
Vancouver, B.C.
Canada V6B 2W9
www.arsenalpulp.com

The publisher gratefully acknowledges the support of the Government of Canada through the Book Publishing Industry Development Program for its publishing activities.

Text design by Lisa Eng-Lodge
Production assistance by Judy Yeung
Cover design by Solo
Front cover photography by Rosalee Hiebert
Interior photography by Brian Wawro and Nicole Bassett
Printed and bound in Canada

The author and publisher assert that the information contained in this book is true and complete to the best of their knowledge. All recommendations are made without guarantee on the part of the author and Arsenal Pulp Press. The author and publisher disclaim any liability in connection with the use of this information. For more information, contact the publisher.

NATIONAL LIBRARY OF CANADA CATALOGUING IN PUBLICATION DATA:
Bassett, Nicole, 1977-
  Chef in your backpack: gourmet cooking in the great outdoors / Nicole Bassett.

  Includes index.
  ISBN 1-55152-140-7

  1. Outdoor cookery. I. Title.
TX823.B37 2003   641.5'782   C2003-910381-1

CONTENTS

ACKNOWLEDGMENTS

Many people contributed their opinions, taste buds, love, and support to make this cookbook come to be. I want to thank:

Emily Kendy, Karen X Tulchinsky, Sachia Kron, Curt Bernardi, Cathleen and Jon Fulton, Brian Wawro, Lee Hoverd, Anthony Del Col, Greg LeClair, Caroline Birks, Ann McGowan, Sandy Walker, Claire Queree, Catherine Crucil, Rosalee Hiebert, Lisa Eng-Lodge, Judy Yeung, The McGowan family, and my family: Keith, Samara, Marley, Monty, Pashan, Agnes, Langie, Bill, and Pat.

I want to thank the people of Arsenal Pulp Press, especially Brian Lam and Blaine Kyllo, for making this book happen.

INTRODUCTION

I got the idea for this book while on a weekend hiking trip with friends in Garibaldi Park in British Columbia. One morning they announced they were going to make pancakes for breakfast. This struck me as rather ambitious; I had always thought that camping food was special for all the wrong reasons: usually dry, not particularly appetizing but high in carbohydrates. But the pancakes they made were great, as good as if they were made at home. And then it occurred to me that there was no reason why camping food had to be bad food; that with a little know-how and creativity, you could eat well while enjoying the great outdoors.

I've always been an outdoors enthusiast. There was no way around it. I grew up on a farm outside Smithers, a small town in northern British Columbia. I spent my childhood surrounded by the beauty of nature, and my parents instilled in me a great love, respect, and appreciation for the environment. In high school, I joined an outdoor education class so that I could hang out with my friends. At the end of the year, we went on a six-day trip to the West Coast Trail on Vancouver Island. During these six days spent being drenched by rain, I went from complete novice to complete wet noodle and vowed to never leave the comforts of home again. However, once we did go home, I could talk of nothing else but the adventures I had. I was hooked. As I got older, I got the bug to spend part of my vacations experiencing different natural surroundings. I've gone hiking and biking around Ireland, Scotland, and Australia, not to mention many great trips in Canada and the U.S. Backcountry skiing, hiking, canoeing, and climbing are such great ways to see the world.

When I was younger, and not the food snob I am today, my outdoor eating experiences left a lot to be desired: Mac and cheese, granola, peanut butter, dried food, and more dried food. Meals became a chore; they were so boring and no longer appetizing. But, I thought, was I overreacting—weren't camping meals supposed to be dull and uninspired? That's part of the camping experience, after all. But now, as every other aspect of camping gear has evolved, it is time for the food to evolve as well. And it can be done with little difficulty.

I've loved cooking ever since I was a kid; I often experimented with food ingredients, creating recipes on my own. After more than a few boring camping meals, and the pancake incident described earlier, I started putting together some of my favorite meals to take on camping trips. They were a huge success; at last, I began to look forward to meals after a long physical day. And boy, were my hiking friends were impressed. Yes, it can be finally said—camping food has changed, for the better!

When it came to compiling recipes for this book, the biggest challenge was coming up with dishes that could be easily made on one stove element, and usually in one pot, light enough to carry but still comprise a full meal. The most important aspect is that the meals should be enjoyable. Hiking all day makes the act of eating all that much more important; the last thing you want after a hard day on the trail is a meal that doesn't taste very good. This means using the freshest ingredients possible, especially since you won't be eating right away (remembering, of course, the dangers of spoilage). It will make your mealtime experiences in the outdoors that much more pleasurable.

In writing this book I have kept in mind that hiking and camping trips can mean a hike, a day-long trek, or a weekend journey. (Again, if your trip is longer, keep in mind that spoilage can be an issue.) And nutrition also plays a role; it's important that the meals you make will provide the kind of fuel you will need while hiking up that mountain or through those trails. Ultimately, it's about good food that doesn't take long to make, is filling, and nutritional.

It was also important for me to keep the recipes as simple as possible and composed of relatively few ingredients that most people already keep on hand in their pantries. I also encourage you to experiment; if you don't like a certain ingredient, take it out (within reason!), or replace it with something you think might work better for you. But beware of replacing any ingredients in the recipes for baked goods; most of these ingredients are essential and the recipes won't work without them.

I believe that food feeds not only the body but the mind as well. The experience of being outdoors and witnessing nature in its absolute beauty feeds us too. The combination of being well-fed, in the company of family and friends, enjoying the sights and sounds of the wilderness, is something that I hold very dear. I hope that *Chef in Your Backpack* adds to your experiences in the great outdoors, and makes your trips more enjoyable and memorable.

HOW TO USE THIS BOOK

In the Kitchen, At Camp

Most recipes are broken down into two parts:

In the Kitchen

In this section are instructions for recipes that are best done at home, before you leave for your trip. These include such activities as cleaning fruits and vegetables, chopping and measuring ingredients, and proper packing instructions. Use zip-lock plastic bags whenever possible; it will keep your food fresher and prevent spillage. Doing these preparations at home will make your meal-making on the trails that much easier.

At Camp

In this section are instructions for once you are in the great outdoors. Hopefully, because you've already done the preliminary work "in the kitchen," all that's left is the actual cooking.

While you can bring this book along with you on your trip, you could also use a felt pen and write down the directions on your plastic bags that contain your ingredients.

Gear

If you intend on hiking to your camping site (as opposed to, say, canoeing or driving), it's imperative that your bags be as light as possible. If you disagree, come with me and you can carry my bag, too! Organizing your gear is very important.

Each recipe is designed with a basic cooking set in mind: one stove and two pots, each with a lid that can be used as a frying pan if so desired, and a clamp handle that allows you to pour liquids easily, which also fits inside the pots when stored. Of course, you can improvise with what you have, but just keep in mind the set I describe allows for minimal weight and fuss.

Also remember to bring dish rags, a scouring pad, and biodegradable soap for doing dishes. Place them in a plastic bag and store inside the pots.

While it would be great to bring along the kitchen stove, you can prepare these recipes with one burner. Most camping stoves only have one burner and are fueled by white gas. The smaller stove you bring, the lighter the load, but you may want to get a more powerful burning stove that will allow you to cook your meals faster. I highly recommend getting a stove equipped with a wind blocker, a piece of aluminum that wraps around the stove to block the wind and thus makes your stove more efficient.

For a lighter load or short trips, you could pare down your eating utensils to a spoon and a cup, depending on what recipes you plan to prepare. But if you have the space, you should take along a cup, bowl, plate, spoon, knife, and fork; it will make your eating that much easier and more enjoyable. I also make great use of my Swiss Army knife, which is good for opening canned goods or slicing and cutting almost anything, including sticks for your marshmallow roasts!

You may wish to consider bringing extra utensils depending on what you've planned for your meals. For instance, a spatula is great if you are making pancakes or French toast.

(You could break off the spatula handle so you don't have to carry as much.) And while a Swiss Army knife is great for any occasion, a separate can opener is easiest for opening canned goods.

Packing

When packing your gear, remember to store the heaviest items at the bottom center of your backpack; this will help with your balance as you hike. Here's an exaggerated analogy: if you were to store pillows at the bottom of your pack and bricks at the top, and then bend over to tie your shoelaces with your backpack on, you'd fall forward (and probably get knocked on the back of the head with your gear, too).

At the same time, food is one of the heaviest items you will be carrying. If you are not carrying a separate food bag (see next page), you don't want to store your food at the bottom of your pack, where it is difficult to reach and might get squashed. Pack your food in the center of your bag, near or at the surface, where it is easily accessible; special snacks, treats, lunch and your water bottle should be packed where they are very accessible.

The Spice Rack

Having spices and condiments at your disposal can make the difference between an okay and a great meal. Empty film canisters are great for storing your spices and condiments; they are easy to transport, and keep your supplies dry. Make up your own spice rack of favorite ingredients and keep it in your food bag (see next page) so you will always have it near; remember to label the canisters so you'll know what they contain. Most of the recipes already include the spices you need (meaning you will have used them at home), so your "take along spice rack" can be very basic, consisting only of those spices and condiments you may want to enhance your meals.

Here are a few to consider including in your spice rack:

Salt	Pepper
Sugar	Garlic powder
Dill	Oregano
Basil	Curry powder
Cumin	

The Food Bag

The food bag is multi-purpose. It's where you should store all items necessary for preparing your meals on your trip: your pots and pans, utensils, dishes, spice rack, and the food itself. Keep these items separate from your other gear, so you will always know where to find your meal-making necessities.

The bag itself should be strong and water-proof (or be prepared to cover it with your pack cover when you are storing your food for the night). Once you have done your meal preparations "in the kitchen," go over the recipe ingredients again to ensure you don't forget anything. Try to split up the food with other members in your group whenever possible, because the load can get heavy pretty fast.

Once you are out in the wilderness, you will need to find a proper place to store your food bag to keep it safe from predators, who may be attracted to it by its smell. The easiest and yet at the same time the most difficult place to store your bag is in a tree. Find a sturdy tree that is away from your tent and cooking area. In addition to food, store any smelly products like toothpaste and deodorant in the bag as well. Then comes the hard part: tie a carabiner (an oblong metal ring with one spring-hinged side, available at outdoors shops) to a rope and swing it up around a branch. Don't worry if you don't make it the first time; it will probably take you a few tries before you get it. Once in place, clip the food bag on, then lift it up and tie it off.

Once you've prepared your food bag once with your basic necessities the first time, it will be easy the next time you take a trip because you already have the basics packed away.

Helpful Tips

• Don't throw away the plastic bags that you use to transport your food in. Rinse them out or just seal and bring them home with you to wash. It's environmentally responsible! (Whenever I refer to plastic bags throughout the book, I mean the resealable zip-lock ones, especially those designed for use in a freezer; they tend to be stronger and more useful for transporting food items.)

• In the recipes where water is required, first pour the water into the plastic bags in order to get any residual spices or oils that might be left behind. It will make your meal that much tastier!

• Some recipes call for canned goods. They will keep longer if you take the cans with you and don't open until you need them. But please clean them out and take them home to recycle!

• Write down the contents of plastic bags or the name of the recipe on the bags themselves. Use a magic marker or felt pen that won't rub out. Nothing's worse than not knowing what's in your bags!

- Thanks to developments in plastic technology, portable egg-carrying cases are available at outdoors stores or department stores. These allow you to bring fresh eggs with you on your trip (but be aware that eggs are considered a "high risk" food and that spoiled eggs are a prime candidate for salmonella poisoning). If you're hiking during summer or other times when the weather is projected to be hot, opt for alternative breakfast ideas.

- Use your camping cup as a measuring cup. Before you leave on your trip, measure a cup of water and place it into your camping cup to see how much it holds. You can then use your cup to measure out liquids on your various trips. Your cup is also useful when preparing rice for cooking. Use 2 cups of water for every 1 cup of rice.

- One big mistake I've made is bringing more food on my treks than I need, thinking that I will be hungrier than my stomach will allow. Before you leave on your trip, get to know yourself and your eating habits, which will allow you to estimate how much food you will need on your trip. If you still aren't sure, try bringing enough food for regular-sized meals and then light extras that you can have just in case you're still hungry, like cheese and crackers, trail mix, muffins, or extra veggies and fruit. If you still end up with too much food, the best thing to do is to return home with it (don't dispose of it on the trails).

Animals

When I was traveling around Australia, where nine of the world's ten most poisonous snakes reside, backpackers often asked me how I could trek around Canadian backcountry "with all those bears." I had just finished thinking the same thing with the snakes and spiders and other creatures lurking around the land of Oz, but I laughed and replied that it is rare if you ever see a bear in the North American wild. In truth, however, they are out there, they are hungry more often than not, and if they smell your food they will want to eat it, without question. If you don't believe me, visit the campground in Banff, Alberta and take a look at the ravaged cooler the rangers have on display as a warning to tourists. Be careful! There are many important guidelines that one must follow when forging into the woods – remember, you are entering the animals' home turf, not vice versa, and learning to cohabitate is best for everyone (and everything) in the long run. Do your research before embarking on any journey, even day trips, as to what dangerous wildlife might be present, and what you should do in the event you encounter something. Think of it this way: would you tease a snake?

Setting Up the Cooking Area

The way you set up your camp is important. If you only keep one thing in mind, make sure that you cook away from your tent. A good distance is about 200 meters (about 650 feet) and down wind. It can be awkward having your cooking area so far away, but it's important to physically separate yourself from what may attract bears and other creatures. With this in mind, it's also vitally important to keep your cooking area clean. Pick up any food that maybe spilled because it only invites critters to come around.

Washing Up

There comes that time in the evening when you're sitting back, your meal sitting nicely in your belly while you watch the stars shoot across the sky, or flames flicker up from the fire pit, and you realize it's your turn to do the dishes. What's the best way? Well, if your meal was so good that everyone licked their plates clean, you're in the clear. If not, store any leftovers in a sealable container, otherwise add it into your garbage that you will take out of the woods with you.

You can use biodegradable soap but remember to keep the soap (or the food, for that matter) away from water sources – streams, rivers, lakes. Fill a pot with water and wash the dishes in the pot. Once you are finished, dig a hole away from your camp and any water source and dump out the dish water. Use a dish rag to dry the dishes.

If you don't have any sponges or scouring pads, use your natural surroundings to aid in dish washing. Sand and snow are excellent for cleaning dishes. When washing, remember to keep a fair distance away from your campsite because the food residue will attract animals.

Store your dishes with your food gear, and not with your camping equipment. Even though the dishes are clean, they still carry an odor that could attract unwanted wildlife. If you want to be extra careful with regard to keeping bears away, don't even bring the clothes you wore while cooking into your tent.

With these tips and suggestions in mind, you should now be ready to embark on your hiking and camping trips confident in the knowledge that it will be a great dining experience. Bon appetit!

Breakfast

I consider breakfast the most important meal of the day, especially when camping, as it is the meal that will set the tone of your entire day. I know it can be difficult to eat substantially in the morning, but your body needs fuel to keep warm and give you enough energy to get you through your busy day (or at least until lunchtime!).

Hot Chocolate from Scratch

½ **cup cocoa powder**
¼ **cup dry milk powder**
⅓ **cup sugar**
Mini-marshallows (optional)
4 cups water

In the Kitchen

In a plastic bag or container, combine all the ingredients, including the marshmallows if desired.

At Camp

Boil the water. Add a couple of tablespoons of the dry mixture and stir well.

Makes 4 servings.

For an extra kick, a splash of Kalua or Irish Cream in your hot chocolate does nicely after a long day of hiking (just remember, "everything in moderation" if you want to be able to hike the next day). You can bring a small – or large – amount in a small plastic water bottle or a bladder.

Breakfast Couscous

1 cup instant couscous
2 tbsp brown sugar
1 tsp cinnamon
pinch ground ginger
½ tsp nutmeg
½ cup fresh berries (e.g., raspberries, blueberries, blackberries or a mixture)
2 cups water

In the Kitchen

In a bowl, combine the couscous, sugar, cinnamon, ginger, nutmeg, and dried berries (if not using fresh; see note below). Place mixture in a resealable plastic bag. Fresh berries should be stored separately.

At Camp

Boil 2 cups of water. Once boiled, add in couscous mixture, cover and let stand for 5 minutes or until all the water has been absorbed, then add fresh berries if using.

Makes 2 servings.

Dried fruit can be used in place of fresh; try raisins, dried cranberries, apples, bananas, or apricots.

Pancakes

¾ cup all-purpose flour
¼ cup powdered egg
2 tbsp dry buttermilk powder
2 tsp sugar
½ tsp baking powder
¾ cup water
2 tsp butter or oil

In the Kitchen

In a bowl, combine all the dry ingredients and store in a plastic bag or container.

At Camp

In a pot, pour in dry mixture and add water. Mix well. In a frying pan or on the lid of your pot, melt butter or oil, then add a scoop of pancake batter and spread out evenly. After edges are cooked, flip pancake until golden.

Makes 2 servings.

Here are some variations on the tried and true pancake:
Cinnamon: Add one teaspoon of cinnamon per cup of dry mix.
Fruit: Add a handful of berries or fruit slices to your wet mix (blueberries work best, but try raspberries, strawberries, bananas)
Chocolate chips: Add two tablespoons to the dry mix

But I need my syrup ...
Use your handy film canisters to carry syrup; place them in zip-lock plastic bags for extra protection. You could also buy small travel containers at the drugstore that one might use for shampoo but are perfectly usable for syrup.

Eggs

I used to think that eggs are the worst possible food to bring hiking because of their fragile nature. But it's possible to enjoy eggs in the great outdoors with a little care and know-how.

Eggs in a bag

Because of the danger of salmonella, it's advisable to use your eggs as soon as possible during your trip. Also, it's best to use them on the cooler days of spring or autumn, and not advisable on hot summer treks. To prevent breakage, crack your eggs at home before you go and place the contents into a strong plastic bag, like ones used for the freezer. For extra safety, place the bag in a second bag and seal.

Omelettes are the easiest (and tastiest) way to prepare eggs in the wild. Into your bag o' eggs add your favorite omelette fixings, like tomatoes, peppers, ham, cheese, onions, and/or mushrooms. If you choose to carry whole eggs, store the omelette ingredients in a separate bag to add to your eggs when you're ready to cook them.

It's easy to burn eggs, so cook them on fairly low heat, and use enough butter, margarine or oil to ensure that your eggs don't stick to your pan.

Alternatively, you can use egg replacers instead of the real thing, especially if you're vegan or have cholesterol issues.

Egg Wraps

4 eggs
2 spinach wraps
1 tbsp butter, margarine or oil
salt and pepper to taste
plus:

Summer Medley
¼ cup cooked ham, diced
¼ cup red or green onions
¼ cup red, green or yellow pepper
¼ cup tomatoes, diced
½ cup cheddar cheese
or:

Brie and Avocado
½ cup Brie cheese, diced
½ cup avocado, diced
or:

Red Pepper Havarti
½ cup roasted red pepper, chopped
½ cup Havarti cheese

In the Kitchen

Crack the eggs and place them in a plastic bag, along with other ingredients depending on the recipe you choose. Store the wraps and the butter or oil separately.

At Camp

In a frying pan or the lid of your pot, heat the butter, margarine or oil. Add the egg mixture and cook like scrambled eggs, making sure they don't burn. Season with salt and pepper. Divide the cooked eggs in two. Place in wraps and roll them up.

Makes 2 servings.

French Toast

¼ cup egg replacer
2 tbsp dried milk powder
½ tsp nutmeg
1 tsp cinnamon
2 tbsp butter, margarine or oil
½ loaf unsliced bread (e.g., a French loaf)
½ cup water

In the Kitchen

Store the egg replacer in a plastic bag.

Combine the milk powder and spices and place in a separate plastic bag. Place the butter, margarine or oil in a film canister.

Cut up the bread into thick slices and store in another plastic bag.

At Camp

In a bowl, combine the eggs and the milk mixture with the water.

In a frying pan or the lid of your pot, heat the butter, margarine or oil. Dip both sides of the bread into the egg mixture and place on the frying pan. Fry one side until golden brown, then flip.

Repeat with rest of the bread. Serve with honey, syrup or jam.

Makes 2 servings.

Hot Fruity Oatmeal

1 cup instant oats
½ tsp cinnamon
½ tsp nutmeg
1 tbsp brown sugar
½ cup dried fruit (e.g., raisins, dried cranberries, dried apricots,
   dried apples, dried peaches, dried bananas)
1 cup water

In the Kitchen

In a bowl combine all the dry ingredients and place in a plastic bag.

At Camp

Boil the water and add it to your oatmeal. How much water really depends on how you like your oatmeal. Let the oatmeal sit for a minute or two so the oats can absorb the water and soften up.

Makes 1 serving.

Designer Granola

4 cups oats
1 cup almond slivers and raw pumpkin seeds, shelled (combined)
1 cup brown sugar
1 tsp cinnamon
⅓ cup canola oil
1 cup dried fruit (e.g., raisins, dried cranberries, dried apples, or a mixture)
¼ cup orange juice
¼ cup milk, water or orange juice (optional)

In the Kitchen

Preheat oven to 350°F (180°C). In a large bowl, combine the oats, almonds, pumpkin seeds, brown sugar, cinnamon, oil, dried fruit, and orange juice. Spread mixture evenly on a cookie sheet and bake for 20 minutes or until golden.

Using a spatula, remove granola in pieces and store in an airtight container. Mix in dried fruit.

Measure out 1-2 cups per person and bring along in a plastic bag.

At Camp

Either combine with milk, water or juice, or simply eat dry (either as part of a meal or as a mid-hike snack).

Makes 6 cups.

Quick & Mighty Muesli

⅓ cup sliced almonds
½ cup bran flakes
¼ cup raw pumpkin seeds, shelled
¾ cup raisins
1 cups rolled oats
2 tbsp sunflower seeds, shelled
¼ cup dried apricots, chopped
¼ cup dried banana chips
2 tbsp brown sugar (optional)
Milk or fruit juice

In the Kitchen

In a frying pan, toast the almonds on dry medium-high heat, stirring often until brown, about 4 minutes. Watch the pan, as they can burn easily. Remove and let cool.

In a bowl, combine the almonds with the remaining ingredients except the milk or fruit juice.

Store in a plastic bag.

At Camp

Combine with milk or fruit juice. The milk can be milk powder reconstituted with water.

Makes 2 servings.

FUN FACTS & TIPS!!!
Plan your trip ahead of time and assign tasks. If someone doesn't like to cook, don't force them; perhaps they could do the dishes or other chores!

Snacks

Eating on the go can be a bit of a challenge. But not only is it good to replenish yourself during your hike, it's also a convenient excuse to stop for a breather and take in the sights. For your mid-hike snacks, you will want something that will give you energy, but in quantities that won't weigh you down and make you feel dozy.

Following here are recipes for ideal for snacks on the go. But you may also wish to bring these simple snacks that require no preparation:

• Apples and nut butter
• Crackers and cheese and/or dried meats
• Dried fruit
• Granola and energy bars
• Rice crackers

Carob & Sunflower Seed Cookies

1 cup whole wheat flour
½ tsp baking soda
½ tsp baking powder
½ tsp salt
½ cup firmly packed brown sugar
½ cup white sugar
½ cup butter or margarine
1 egg
1 tsp vanilla extract
1 tbsp milk or soy milk
1 cup uncooked quick rolled oats
⅔ cup mixed seeds (e.g., sunflower, sesame, pumpkin)
½ cup carob or chocolate chips

In the Kitchen

Preheat oven to 350°F (180°C) and grease two cookie sheets.

In a medium bowl, combine the flour, baking soda, baking powder, and salt.

In a large bowl, cream the sugars with butter or margarine, then add egg, vanilla, and milk and combine until smooth. Gradually add in flour mixture until blended.

Add oats, seeds, and carob chips.

Spoon out onto cookie sheets and bake for 10-12 minutes or until golden brown.

Store in an air-tight container.

Makes approx. 24 cookies.

Muesli Bars

3 cups muesli (store-bought, or see page 24)
4 tbsp sunflower oil
4 tbsp honey
1 tsp allspice
1 egg (beaten)
2 tbsp brown sugar

In the Kitchen

Preheat oven to 325°F (160°C).

Grease shallow baking tin and line with wax paper (7"x11").

In a bowl, combine all the ingredients and spoon evenly into the pan until it is level.

Bake for 30-35 minutes until light brown around the edges. Remove, cool slightly, and with the tip of a knife mark into 12-16 pieces.

Cool completely, turn out onto a wire rack, and break into marked pieces.

Store in an air-tight container.

Makes 12-16 bars.

Trail Mix

Trail mix is that old hiking stand-by, traditionally made of dried fruits and nuts. Trail mix gives you that burst of energy when you need it most; it tastes great, and it will keep your blood sugars up. By making your own, you can be sure to include ingredients that you want yourself. But use these ideas as a guide, and be creative!

Fruit

Raisins, currants, saltanas, dried bananas, dried apricots, dried papayas, dried mangoes, dried apples, dried cranberries, dried cherries, prunes, dates.

Nuts

Cashews, peanuts, almonds, walnuts, soy nuts, pecans, hazelnuts. For a variation, try toasting them before adding to your trail mix. Preheat the oven to 200°F (100°C). Arrange nuts evenly on a cookie sheet and bake for about 5 minutes or until brown. Watch them so they don't burn.

Goodies

Chocolate chips are a nice sweet addition; there are all sorts of flavors available now, including raspberry, mint, butterscotch, and peanut butter, to name a few. Or try carob chips, macaroons, or candy like Rosebuds, Smarties, or M&Ms or Reese's Pieces.

Sweet and Spice Popcorn & Nuts

⅔ cup unpopped popcorn

¾ cup peanuts and or pecans

½ cup melted butter or margarine

½ cup honey, molasses, or maple syrup

1 tbsp Spike or Greek seasoning salt

In the Kitchen

Preheat oven to 350°F (180°C).

Pop the popcorn and combine in a large bowl with the nuts.

In a pot over medium heat, combine the butter or margarine and honey or molasses or maple syrup. Bring mixture to a boil, then continue stirring for 10 minutes.

Pour mixture over the popcorn and nuts, and toss with Spike seasoning salt. Spread evenly on a large baking pan and bake for 15 minutes. Stir mixture a couple of times during baking. Remove and cool.

Store in an air-tight container or bring along in personal-sized bags for eating while hiking.

Makes 4 cups.

Spike and Greek seasoning salt are pre-mixed spices available at most grocery stores.

Protein Bars

1 cup brown sugar

½ cup margarine, softened

1 tsp vanilla extract

1 egg

½ cup orange juice

½ cup whole wheat flour

½ cup wheat germ or bran

¼ tsp salt

½ cup protein or soy powder

1 cup oats

1 cup dried fruit or chocolate or carob chips

¼ cup pecans

In the Kitchen

Preheat oven to 350°F (180°C).

In a large bowl, cream the sugar, margarine, vanilla, and egg together.

In a separate bowl, combine the rest of the ingredients and mix well.

Stir into creamed mixture and mix well.

Spread evenly on a greased 9"x12" pan and bake for 30-40 minutes. Cool and cut into bars.

Makes 12 bars.

FUN FACTS & TIPS!!!

Paint by numbers: use differently colored bags and packs so you'll know where certain things are.

Hiker Delight Cookies

¾ cup whole wheat flour
1 cup bran (or cereal)
½ cup rolled oats
½ tsp baking soda
¼ tsp salt
½ tsp nutmeg
1 tsp cinnamon
¼ tsp cloves
½ cup butter or margarine
¾ cup brown sugar
1 egg
1 tsp vanilla extract
½ cup dried apricots, chopped
¼ cup raisins
¼ cup nuts (any kind)

In the Kitchen

Preheat oven to 350°F (180°C) and grease cookie sheets.

In a small bowl, combine the flour, bran, baking soda, salt, nutmeg, cinnamon, and cloves.

In a larger bowl, cream the butter and sugar together. Once fluffy, beat in the egg and vanilla. Add the dry ingredients a bit at a time and mix until blended. Stir in apricots, raisins, and nuts.

Spoon out portions onto cookie sheets and bake for 10-12 minutes until brown.

Makes approx. 24 cookies.

Puff Rice Squares

⅓ **cup honey or maple syrup**
¼ **cup packed brown sugar**
⅓ **cup butter or margarine**
6 cups puffed wheat or rice or kamut cereal

In the Kitchen

Grease a 9"x9" baking pan.

In a medium saucepan over medium heat, combine the margarine, maple syrup, and brown sugar. Stir often until mixture comes to a boil. Continue boiling for 1 minute, then remove from heat.

In a large bowl, place the puffed wheat. Pour liquid mixture over it and stir until evenly coated. Press the mixture evenly into the greased pan. Let cool and cut into squares.

Makes 12 squares.

For hiking, wrap each square individually so they don't stick together.

Ginger Snap Cookies

2¼ cups all-purpose flour
1 tsp baking soda
1 tsp ground cinnamon
½ tsp ground cloves
¼ tsp salt
¼ tsp black pepper
¾ cup margarine or butter, softened
1 cup brown sugar
1 egg
¼ cup molasses
1 tbsp water
3 tbsp fresh ginger, grated
¼ cup white sugar (for rolling)

In the Kitchen

Preheat oven to 350°F (180°C).

Sift together the flour, baking soda, cinnamon, cloves, salt, and pepper. Set aside.

In a large bowl, cream the margarine and brown sugar together until light and fluffy. Add the egg and beat well, then stir in water, molasses, and ginger. Gradually stir in the dry ingredients.

Roll the dough into walnut-sized balls and roll them in the white sugar.

On an ungreased cookie sheet, place the cookies two inches apart and flatten slightly with the bottom of a glass.

Makes 24 cookies.

**FUN
FACTS & TIPS!!!**
Old shower curtains
make good
ground clothes.

Health Fruit Bars

2 cups puffed rice
1½ cups rolled oats
¼ cup sunflower seeds, shelled
¼ cup sesame seeds
1 cup mixed dried fruit, chopped (e.g., raisins, dried cranberries,
   dried apricots, dried apples, dried bananas)
⅓ cup rice flour
½ cup peanut butter
½ cup maple syrup
¼ cup honey
½ carob or chocolate chips

In the Kitchen

Preheat oven to 350°F (175°C).

Line the base and up the lengthwise sides of an 8"x12" baking tin with wax paper.

In a large bowl, combine the puffed rice, rolled oats, sunflower and sesame seeds, dried fruit, and rice flour and mix well.

In a small saucepan over medium heat, combine the peanut butter, maple syrup, and honey and heat gently for 2 minutes or until it becomes runny. Add the liquid mixture to the dry ingredients and mix until coated.

Using a piece of wax paper to protect your fingers, press the mixture firmly into the prepared pan and spread it evenly. Bake for 15 minutes or until golden brown.

Remove and let cool and crisp in tin before cutting it into bars. Store in an air-tight container.

Makes 20 bars.

Peach Apricot Oat Bars

Crust:
2½ cups rolled oats
1 cup whole wheat flour
1 cup packed brown sugar
1 tsp baking powder
1 tsp cinnamon
½ tsp salt
1 cup shortening or margarine

Filling:
¾ cup dried apricots
1 14-oz (398-ml) can peaches
2 tbsp lemon juice (fresh preferable)

In the Kitchen

Preheat oven to 350°F (175°C). Grease a 9"x9" square baking pan.

For the crust: in a large bowl, combine the rolled oats, flour, brown sugar, baking powder, cinnamon, and salt. Cut in shortening or margarine until mixture becomes crumbly (use your hands to do this, or a pastry cutter).

For the filling: in a medium pot over medium high heat, combine the apricots and peaches and cook until thick. Remove from heat and stir in lemon juice.

Press half of the crust mixture evenly into baking pan. Spread fruit mixture over top. Crumble rest of crust mixture over top of the fruit. Bake for 20-25 minutes. Let cool before cutting into bars.

Makes approx. 12 bars.

These are great for a mid-hike snack or an after-dinner dessert.

Lemon Strawberry Oat Bars

Crust:

2½ cups rolled oats

1 cup whole wheat flour

1 cup packed brown sugar

1 tsp baking powder

1 tsp cinnamon

½ tsp salt

1 cup shortening or margarine

Filling:

1 cup sugar

3 tbsp all-purpose flour

¼ tsp baking powder

3 eggs

½ cup lemon juice (fresh preferable)

1 cup strawberries, cut into small chunks

In the Kitchen

Preheat oven to 350°F (175°C). Grease a 9"x9" square baking pan.

For the crust: in a large bowl, combine the rolled oats, flour, brown sugar, baking powder, cinnamon, and salt. Cut in shortening or margarine until mixture becomes crumbly (use your hands to do this, or a pastry cutter).

For filling: in a medium bowl, combine all the ingredients, adding the strawberries last, and mix well.

Press half of the crust mixture evenly into baking pan. Spread fruit mixture over top.

Bake for 10 minutes, then remove from oven and add the rest of the crust mixture on top. Return to oven and bake for another 15 minutes until brown. Let cool before cutting into bars.

Makes approx. 12 bars.

Sugar & Spice Nuts

1 egg white
2 cups unsalted mixed nuts (e.g., peanuts, cashews,
    walnuts, peacans, almonds, etc.)
½ tsp canola oil
⅓ cup brown sugar
½ tsp cinnamon
¼ tsp nutmeg
¼ tsp cayenne pepper
½ tsp salt

In the Kitchen

Preheat oven to 325°F (160°C).

Beat egg white until foamy.

In a large bowl, combine nuts with egg and oil until coated. Stir in the remaining ingredients and toss well until coated.

Spread out on a baking sheet and bake for about 15 minutes, stirring often, until golden. Remove and cool completely before using.

Store in an air-tight container or zip-lock plastic bag.

Makes 2 cups.

Tofu Sticks

1 pkg extra firm tofu
½ cup Braggs sauce (see note below)

In the Kitchen

Preheat oven to 350°F (175°C).

Cut tofu into rectangular slices.

In a baking dish, marinate the tofu slices in the Braggs for 1 hour. After 30 minutes, turn the slices over so both sides will absorb the Braggs.

Bake for 20 minutes, turning over tofu slices after 10 minutes so that they are browned on all sides.

Cool and store in an air-tight container or zip-lock plastic bag.

Makes 12 sticks.

These tofu sticks are a savory protein-packed snack.

Braggs is a tamari/soy sauce alternative that is neither heated, fermented, nor salted. It's available in health food stores and better grocery stores.

Cranberry & White Chocolate Biscotti

2 cups all-purpose flour
1½ tsp baking powder
¼ tsp salt
½ cup butter or margarine, softened
¾ cup white sugar
2 eggs
1 tsp vanilla extract
½ cup dried cranberries
½ cup white chocolate chips
½ cup hazelnuts, chopped

In the Kitchen

Preheat oven to 350°F (180°C). Grease and flour a cookie sheet.

In a medium bowl, combine the flour, baking powder, and salt and mix well.

In a large bowl, cream the butter or margarine and sugar together until fluffy. Add the eggs and vanilla and mix until well blended. Gradually stir in flour mixture. Stir in cranberries, white chocolate chips, and hazelnuts.

Divide dough into two equal parts. On a floured surface, shape the dough into two logs, about 2 inches across and 1 inch thick. Place the logs 2 inches apart on the prepared cookie sheet.

Bake for 25 minutes or until lightly browned. Remove and let cool for 5 minutes, then cut into ¾ inch slices. Return to cookie sheet standing slices up right.

Return to oven and bake for an additional 10 minutes, until slightly dry. Remove and let cool.

Makes 16 biscotti.

Biscotti makes for a nice treat, either with your lunch or as a dessert for you to dip in your hot chocolate, tea or coffee at the end of the day. They also make for a nice, light, and fancy breakfast.

Mixed Cereal Squares

¼ cup margarine
1 15-oz (250-g) pkg marshmallows
1 tsp vanilla extract
6 cups mixed cereal (see note below)
½ cup dried fruit, chopped (e.g., raisins, dried apricots,
  dried cranberries) (optional)

In the Kitchen

Grease a 9"x12" baking pan.

In a large pot over medium heat, combine the margarine and marshmallows until melted and smooth. Turn off the heat and add the vanilla.

Stir in the cereal and dried fruit until completely coated.

Pour mixture into the baking pan and spread out.

Let cool and cut into squares.

In order to remain somewhat healthy on your hike, choose high fiber and mixed grain cereals like bran or corn flakes, rolled oats, or museli, among others.

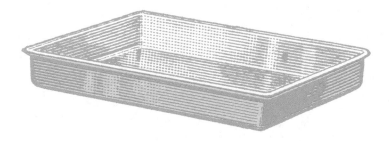

Chocolate Chocolate Chip Cookies

2½ cups all-purpose flour
1 tsp baking soda
½ tsp salt
3 tbsp cocoa powder
1 cup butter or margarine, softened
1 cup brown sugar, firmly packed
½ cup white sugar
2 tsp vanilla extract
2 eggs
2 cups chocolate chips

In the Kitchen

Preheat the oven to 375°F (190°C).

In a small bowl, combine the flour, baking soda, salt, and cocoa powder.

In a large bowl, cream the butter and brown sugar together. Add the white sugar and mix, then the vanilla, then the eggs and mix until smooth. Slowly add in the flour and mix until absorbed.

Add the chocolate chips.

Spoon mixture onto an ungreased cookie sheet. Bake for 8-10 minutes, until cookies are dark brown on the bottom.

Remove from cookie sheet and let cool.

Makes 24 cookies.

With cocoa powder and chocolate chips, you double the chocolate and hence double your energy!

Banana Nut Muffins

2 cups whole wheat flour
1 tbsp baking powder
½ tsp salt
½ cup honey
¼ cup vegetable oil
2 eggs, beaten
⅔ cup skim or soy milk
1½ cups bananas, mashed
½ cup walnuts, chopped

In the Kitchen

Preheat oven to 400°F (200°C).

Grease muffin pan or line with paper muffin cups.

Sift together the flour, baking powder, and salt. In a bowl, combine the honey, oil, eggs, milk, and bananas and then mix into flour mixture with a couple of swift strokes. Fold in the nuts.

Pour mixture into muffin pan until about ¾ full.

Bake for 20-25 minutes, until brown on top, and a toothpick inserted comes out clean.

Cool and store in an air-tight container.

Makes 12 muffins.

Muffins make a great snack; you can load them up with all kinds of goodies that will give you energy on your trip. It can also be a great source of extra fruit or fiber, depending on your ingredients.

If your bananas start to go brown, place them in the freezer. If you need mashed bananas (as in this recipe), simply remove them from the freezer, pop them in the microwave to thaw, and then use.

Berry Bran Muffins

2 cups whole wheat flour
1½ tsp baking soda
¼ tsp salt
1½ cups wheat bran
3 tbsp butter, margarine or oil
2 tbsp brown sugar
1-2 tbsp orange rind, grated
½ cup molasses
1 egg
2 cups milk, buttermilk or soy milk
1 cup berries (e.g., blueberries, raspberries, blackberries)

In the Kitchen

Preheat oven to 350°F (180°C).

Grease muffin pan or line with paper muffin cups.

Sift together the flour, baking soda and salt. Add the bran and mix well.

In a medium bowl, beat the butter with the sugar, orange rind, and molasses until well mixed. Add the egg and milk. Add the flour mixture and mix well with as few strokes as possible. Add the berries.

Pour into muffin tin until about ¾ full.

Bake for 25 minutes, until brown on top, and a toothpick inserted comes out clean.

Cool and store in an air-tight container.

Makes 12 muffins.

FUN FACTS & TIPS!!!
If you are planning a hiking trip into the mountains, remember that as you gain altitude, food takes longer to cook, so plan meals that are quicker to make.

Zucchini Spice Muffins

1 cup all-purpose flour

1¼ cups whole wheat or rye flour

1 tsp baking soda

1½ tsp baking powder

2 tsp ground cinnamon

½ tsp ground ginger

2 tsp ground cloves

2 tsp nutmeg

½ tsp salt

½ cup walnut pieces or chocolate or carob chips (optional)

¾ cup vegetable oil or melted margarine

1 cup brown sugar

2 eggs

½ cup milk, buttermilk or soy milk

2 cups zucchini, grated

In the Kitchen

Preheat oven to 350°F (180°C).

Grease muffin pan or line with paper muffin cups.

In a medium bowl, combine the flours, baking soda, baking powder, cinnamon, ginger, cloves, nutmeg, salt, and walnuts, and mix well.

In a separate medium bowl, combine the oil or margarine, sugar, eggs, milk, and zucchini.

Add the wet ingredients to the dry and mix until combined.

Pour into muffin pan until about ¾ full.

Bake for 20-25 minutes, until brown on top, and a toothpick inserted comes out clean.

Cool and store in an air-tight container.

Makes 12 muffins.

Lemon Poppyseed Muffins

2 cups all-purpose flour
¾ cup white sugar
1 tbsp baking powder
½ tsp salt
1 tbsp lemon zest, grated
¼ cup poppyseeds
½ cup milk
⅓ cup vegetable oil or melted margarine
1 egg
⅓ cup lemon juice (fresh preferred)

In the Kitchen

Preheat oven to 350°F (175°C).

Grease muffin pan or line with paper muffin cups.

In a medium bowl, combine the flour, sugar, baking powder, salt, lemon zest, and poppyseeds, and mix well.

In a small bowl, combine the milk, oil or margarine, lemon juice, and egg, and mix well.

Add the wet ingredients to the dry, and mix together with a few quick strokes until combined.

Pour into muffin pan until about ¾ full.

Bake for 20-25 minutes, until golden on top and a toothpick inserted comes out clean.

Cool and store in an air-tight container.

Makes 12 muffins.

Raspberry Pecan Muffins

2 cups whole wheat flour
1 cup wheat bran
½ cup oat bran
1½ tsp baking soda
2 tsp baking powder
½ tsp salt
1½ tsp cinnamon
1 cup packed brown sugar
½ cup butter or margarine, melted
2 eggs
1½ cups plain yogurt
¾ cup whole pecans, toasted
1½ cup raspberries

In the Kitchen

Preheat oven to 375°F (190°C).

Grease muffin pan or line with paper muffin cups.

In a large bowl, combine the flour, wheat bran, oat bran, baking soda, baking powder, salt, cinnamon, and sugar, and mix well.

In a medium bowl, combine the butter or margarine, yogurt, and eggs, and mix well.

Add the wet ingredients to the dry, and mix together until combined. Add the pecans and raspberries.

Pour into muffin pan until about ¾ full.

Bake for 20-25 minutes, until golden on top and a toothpick inserted comes out clean.

Cool and store in an air-tight container.

Makes 12 muffins.

Carrot Muffins

2 cups whole wheat flour
2 tsp baking soda
1½ tsp cinnamon
½ tsp ground ginger
¼ tsp salt
1¼ brown sugar
2 cups carrots, grated
½ cup walnuts
½ cup raisins
3 large eggs
1 cup butter or margarine, melted
2 tsp vanilla extract

In the Kitchen

Preheat oven to 350°F (180°C).

Grease muffin pan or line with paper muffin cups.

In a large bowl, combine the flour, baking soda, cinnamon, ginger, salt, and sugar and mix well. Add the carrots, walnuts, and raisins and mix well.

In a medium bowl, whisk the eggs together with the butter or margarine and vanilla.

Add the wet ingredients to the dry, and mix together until combined. Pour into muffin pan until about ¾ full.

Bake for 20-25 minutes, until golden on top and a toothpick inserted comes out clean.

Cool and store in an air-tight container.

Makes 12 muffins.

Lunch

Every meal is important, but when you're hiking, lunch becomes even more so; it's vital that you take the time to re-fuel. If you are planning lunch for a day hike, or the first lunch on a multi-day trek, you could bring almost anything you want, provided it's easily portable. Enjoy the foods you probably will not be having for a few days because they spoil quickly; look at it as your last meal. But whether it's your first day or your third, there are lots of great things you can bring along for your noon-time eats.

Keep in mind that in addition to the ideas presented in this chapter, recipes in the dinner chapter can also be prepared for lunch, provided you have time to set up your stove and cook. You can also plan on eating leftovers from the night before for lunch; just remember to bring along a container to store them in.

The salads in this chapter can be enjoyed by two as a large-portion lunch, or if used as an accompaniment, they can be shared by more than two people. For example, a salad served with a sandwich, or two different salads, can provide lunch for four people.

Best PB&J Sandwiches

I know what you're thinking — a recipe for peanut butter and jelly sandwiches? Even a monkey can make a good one. But here's how to make a great one!

- Try organic peanut butter for a change. Heck, get rid of the peanut butter altogether and go for another nut butter: almond, walnut, cashew, and other nut butters are all available at your local health food store and many grocery stores. They make a nice alternative to the standard peanut.

- Spread the peanut butter on both slices of bread, and then the jam on one slice. This prevents the jam from making your bread soggy.

- Jams or jellies come in various flavors, but if you want to step outside the realm of PB&J, try honey, Nutella (the brand-name hazelnut and cocoa spread), or bananas instead of (or in addition to) jam or jelly. If you are bringing condiments to use on the trail, you should transfer them out of their jars and bring only what you think you will need; this will make your load easier and lighter.

- There are squeezable tubes that can be purchased at most outdoors stores; use these to load up your peanut butter, jam, or other condiments, then squeeze out what you need.

Best Tuna Sandwiches

1 6-oz (170-g) can solid white tuna
½ cup feta cheese, crumbled
¼ cup Kalamata olives, pitted and sliced
½ cup spinach, chopped
¼ tsp black pepper
Foccacia or rye bread, sliced

In the Kitchen

In a bowl, combine the tuna, cheese, olives, spinach, and pepper and mix well. Store in a plastic bag.

At Camp

Spread the mixture on the bread and serve.

Makes 2 sandwiches.

Sautéed Veggie Sandwiches

¾ cup red peppers, chopped
½ cup zucchini, chopped
⅔ cup mushrooms, chopped
¼ cup red onions, chopped
1 tbsp olive oil
1 tsp balsamic vinegar
½ tsp dried oregano
½ tsp dried rosemary
salt and pepper to taste
Monterey Jack cheese
Foccacia or rye bread, sliced

In the Kitchen

In a medium saucepan over medium high heat, sauté the vegetables together with oil, vinegar, oregano, rosemary, salt, and pepper until soft. Remove from heat and let cool. Store in a plastic bag.

At Camp

Construct sandwiches with the vegetables, cheese, and bread.

Makes 2 sandwiches.

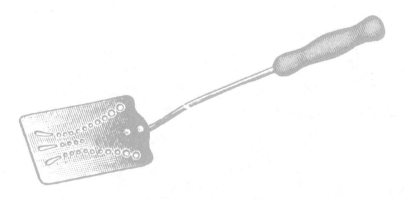

Lentil Burger Pitas

1 cup dried lentils
1 egg
½ pkg dry onion soup mix
½ cup cornmeal
1 tbsp olive oil
2 pita breads
2 tbsp hummus
Lettuce leaves
½ green or red bell pepper, sliced
Alfalfa sprouts

In the Kitchen

In a bowl of water, soak the lentils overnight.

Drain the lentils. In a pot over high heat, boil the lentils in 4 cups of water for approximately 20 minutes, until soft. Remove from heat, drain, and let cool.

In a medium bowl, combine the egg, onion soup mix, and cornmeal and mix well.

Add the lentils to the egg mixture. Roll mixture into uniform balls, then flatten to form patties.

On a non-stick frying pan over medium heat, fry the patties on both sides until crisp. Set aside to cool.

At Camp

Construct your burger pita with the lettuce, humus, peppers, and sprouts.

Makes 4 sandwiches.

Instead of pitas, use your favorite sandwich-making bread, or even bagels.

Smoked Turkey & Pesto Sandwiches

½ roasted yellow bell pepper, sliced
4 tbsp pesto (see page 96)
½ loaf French bread, sliced
20 oz (50 g) smoked turkey breast slices
1 medium bocconcini cheese, sliced
½ cup arugula, chopped

In the Kitchen

Roast the pepper: Preheat oven to 350°F (180°C). Place pepper on oven rack for 10 minutes, then turn over and do the same on the other side. Place in a bowl and cover with plastic wrap. Once cool, peel the skin and slice into strips.

Spread pesto on bread slices. Top with peppers, turkey, cheese, and arugula.

Wrap sandwiches well and eat for that day's lunch.

Makes 2 sandwiches.

If bocconcini cheese isn't available, you can use any mozzarella.

Great Breads

Having the right kind of bread can make a world of difference to your sandwich. There are lots to choose from; in addition to these, try new ones you find at your favorite bakery. Just remember that breads are easily squashed in your backpack, so here are examples of some good breads that pack well.

Pumpernickel

What's so great about a bread that weighs a ton? It will be able to handle your trek intact, for one thing! This is a heavy, hearty bread good for sandwiches with lots of ingredients.

Pita bread

A good flatbread that is light and a great companion with dinner. Also great for stuffing with salads and other fixings for lunch.

Turkish bread and other flat breads

Usually made of flour, oil, and water, flat breads are great because there's no possibility of them getting flatter while hiking! They work well with dips.

Bagels

Bagels are a great addition to your camping lunches. They provide carbohydrates for your body and because they are fairly heavy, they don't get too squashed in your backpack. Bagels come in different flavors: yummy cheese, onion, raisin, multigrain, or whatever your fancy. You can get store-bought, or make your own, especially if you have a breadmaker at home.

Toppings are up to you, but here are some favorites:
• peanut or other nut butters
• cream cheese (lots of different flavors available)
• lox (smoked salmon)
• deli meats
• deli cheeses
• vegetables (raw or roasted)
• Hummus (page 58), Eggplant Dip (page 59), White Bean Dip (page 60)

My Mom's Cornbread

¼ cup margarine or butter
1 cup cornmeal
1 cup flour
½ tsp salt
4 tsp baking powder
¼ cup white sugar or honey
1 egg
1 cup milk

In the Kitchen

Preheat oven to 425°F (210°C).

In an 8"x8" pan, melt the margarine or butter in the oven. Watch that it doesn't burn.

In a bowl, combine the cornmeal, flour, baking powder, sugar, and salt. Add in the egg and milk and mix well.

Add the mixture to the pan with the melted margarine. Bake for 20-25 minutes.

Every time my mom made this cornbread, it was gone before it even had a chance to cool. It's a sweet, moist bread that is great any time of the day.

FUN FACTS & TIPS!!!
Use previously used campsites when available rather than create one of your own, to decrease your impact on terrain.

Hummus Dip

1 19-oz (538-ml) can garbanzo beans (chickpeas), including liquid
3 tbsp lemon juice
6 tbsp tahini (see note below)
1 tbsp olive oil
3 cloves garlic, crushed
¼ tsp chili powder
salt and pepper to taste

In the Kitchen

In a blender or food processor, purée all the ingredients except for the parsley. Pour mixture into a plastic container.

This dip and those that follow can be used with veggies or crackers, or as a spread on breads or bagels.

Fresh raw vegetables are easy to carry and make a great on-the-go snack. Chop them up and store in zip-lock plastic bags. Popular veggies for these dips include carrots, zucchini, celery, green beans, snow peas, broccoli, and cauliflower.

Tahini is a smooth paste made from sesame seeds.

Eggplant Dip

2 medium eggplants
¼ cup onion, chopped
2 garlic cloves
1 tbsp olive oil
2 tbsp lemon juice
¼ tsp salt
¼ tsp pepper

In the Kitchen

Preheat oven to 400°F (200°C).

Poke holes in the eggplants with a fork and bake on a baking sheet for 20 minutes until eggplants become soft. When cool, remove the skin and roughly chop.

In a blender or food processor, purée the eggplant with the onions, garlic, oil, lemon juice, salt, and pepper. Place in a plastic container.

White Bean Dip

1 14-oz (396-ml) can navy beans, drained
2 tbsp lemon juice
1 tbsp tamari (see note below)
¼ tsp cayenne pepper
½ green pepper
1 garlic clove
1 tbsp olive oil

In the Kitchen

In a food processor or blender, purée all the ingredients. Pour into a plastic container.

Tamari is an aged soy sauce found in Asian markets and better grocery stores.

Curry Lentil Dip

1 14-oz (396-ml) can lentils, including liquid
½ red pepper, chopped
1 tbsp curry powder
1 tsp cumin
½ tsp coriander
1 clove garlic, minced
1 tsp fresh ginger, minced
¼ tsp black pepper
1 tbsp olive oil

In the Kitchen

In a food processor or blender, purée all the ingredients. Pour into a plastic container.

Summer Garden Lentil Salad

1 cob of corn, kernels removed
¼ cup green onions, chopped
¾ cup cucumber, chopped
⅔ cup tomato, chopped
1 14-oz (396-ml) can lentils, drained and rinsed
1 tbsp olive oil
2 tbsp balsamic vinegar
2 tbsp fresh basil, chopped
salt and pepper to taste

In the Kitchen

In a pot of boiling water, cook the corn for 10 minutes. Once cooled, cut off the kernels and add to the rest of the chopped vegetables.

In a bowl, combine the vegetables, lentils, oil, and vinegar and mix well. Store in a plastic container or plastic bag.

At Camp

Season with salt and pepper to taste before serving. Serve on its own or as an accompaniment.

Makes 2 servings.

FUN FACTS & TIPS!!!
If the weather is cold, exercise for a few minutes before climbing into your sleeping bag. You will give off heat and warm up your bag, making it more comfortable to sleep in.

Orange Lentil Salad

1 14-oz (396-ml) can lentils, drained
2 tbsp fresh mint, finely chopped
1 cup cucumber, chopped
2 medium oranges

In the Kitchen

In a bowl, combine the lentils, mint, and cucumber and mix well.

Squeeze the juice of 1 orange over the lentils. Chop up the remaining orange into pieces and add to salad.

Store in a plastic container or plastic bag.

At Camp

Serve on its own or as an accompaniment.

Makes 2 servings.

Tabbouleh Salad

1 cup bulgur (see note below)
1 cup boiling water
1 cup cucumber, chopped
½ cup tomato, chopped
1 clove garlic, minced
½ cup parsley, minced
⅔ cup carrot, shredded
¼ cup green onions, chopped
1 tbsp olive oil
2 tbsp lemon juice
2 tbsp lime juice
2 tbsp fresh mint, chopped
salt and pepper to taste

In the Kitchen

In a bowl, pour boiling water over the bulgur. Let stand for 15 minutes, or until all the water has been absorbed.

Add the vegetables to the softened bulgur and mix well. Add the oil, lemon juice, lime juice, and mint and mix well.

Store in a plastic container or plastic bag.

At Camp

Season with salt and pepper to taste. Serve on its own, or stuffed into pita breads, or as an accompaniment.

Makes 2 servings.

Bulgur is a parched cracked wheat that is a staple of this popular salad. It's available in grocery stores or health food stores.

Sweet Chickpea Salad

1 14-oz (396-ml) can garbanzo beans (chickpeas), drained
1 cup mango, diced
½ cup cucumber, chopped
2 tbsp lime juice
½ cup red pepper, chopped
2 tbsp fresh parsley, chopped
pinch cayenne pepper
¼ tsp salt
¼ tsp pepper

In the Kitchen

In a bowl, combine all the ingredients and mix well. Store in a plastic container or plastic bag.

At Camp

Serve on its own or as an accompaniment.

Makes 2 servings.

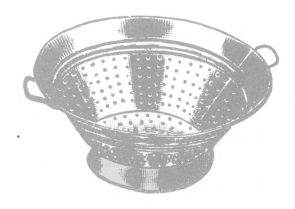

Jerk Tuna & Chickpea Salad

Jerk seasoning:
1 tsp dried thyme
1 tsp paprika
1 tsp brown sugar
¼ tsp dried mustard
¼ tsp ground cumin
¼ tsp salt
½ tsp black pepper
cayenne pepper to taste

1 6-oz (170-g) can solid white tuna packed in water, drained
1 19-oz (538-ml) can garbanzo beans (chickpeas), drained
¼ cup green onions, chopped
1 cup red and green bell peppers, chopped
2 tbsp parsley, chopped

In the Kitchen

For the seasoning: In a bowl, combine all the ingredients and mix well. Add the cayenne pepper to taste; add slowly, taste, then add a bit more if necessary for a spicier mix.

In a separate bowl, combine the tuna, chickpeas, green onions, peppers, and parsley and mix well. Add the seasoning and mix well.

Store in a plastic container or plastic bag.

At Camp

Serve on its own or as an accompaniment.

Makes 2 servings.

FUN FACTS & TIPS!!!
Devise a camp washing machine with a large bucket and a toilet plunger.

Salsa Pasta Salad

2 cups cooked rotini pasta
1 cup tomatoes, chopped
1 cob of corn, kernels removed
½ cup green bell pepper, chopped
¼ cup red onions, chopped
1 tsp red pepper flakes
⅓ cup fresh cilantro, chopped
1 tsp olive oil
juice of 1 lime
¼ tsp salt
¼ tsp pepper
¼ cup cheddar cheese, grated (optional)

In the Kitchen

Cook the pasta, rinse, and allow to cool to at least room temperature.

In a pot of boiling water, cook the corn for 10 minutes. Once cooled, cut off the kernels and add to the rest of the chopped vegetables.

In a bowl, combine the vegetables with the red pepper flakes, cilantro, oil, lime juice, salt, and pepper and mix well. Let sit to marinate.

In a large bowl, combine the cooked pasta and salsa and mix well. Store in a plastic container.

At Camp

Sprinkle with cheddar cheese if desired. Serve on its own or as an accompaniment.

Makes 2 servings.

Prosciutto Pasta Salad

2 cups cooked shell pasta
8 stalks asparagus, chopped
¼ cup green onions, chopped
1 cup yellow bell pepper, chopped
¼ lb proscuitto, diced
2 tbsp oilve oil
2 tbsp balsamic vinegar
1 tsp Dijon mustard
½ tsp dried dill
¼ cup Parmesan cheese, grated

In the Kitchen

Cook the pasta, rinse, and allow to cool to at least room temperature.

In a pot of boiling water, blanch the asparagus for a few minutes, then rinse under cold water.

In a large bowl, combine the cooked pasta, asparagus, green onions, bell peppers, and proscuitto and mix well.

In a small bowl, combine the oil, vinegar, mustard, and dill. Beat with a fork for 1 minute until smooth.

Pour the dressing over the pasta and mix well.

At Camp

Toss with Parmesan cheese. Serve on its own or as an accompaniment.

Makes 2 servings.

Proscuitto ham is an Italian cured ham available at your favorite deli counter.

Festive Couscous Salad

¾ cup couscous
1 cup boiling water
½ cup dried cranberries
½ cup roasted peanuts
¾ cup green bell pepper, chopped
2 tbsp parsley, chopped
2 tbsp lime juice
4 tbsp honey
1 tsp sesame oil

In the Kitchen

In a bowl, pour boiling water over the couscous, cover and let stand until all the water has been absorbed.

In a large bowl, combine the softened couscous, cranberries, peanuts, bell peppers, and parsley.

In a small bowl, combine the lime, honey, and oil and mix well. Pour over couscous mixture.

Store in a plastic container.

At Camp

Serve on its own or as an accompaniment.

Makes 2 servings.

FUN FACTS & TIPS!!!
Remember to take breaks from your hike for a snack and a drink of water; a little fuel in the tank with help you keep moving and alert.

Orzo Salad

2 cups cooked orzo pasta
1 14-oz (396-ml) can garbanzo beans (chickpeas), drained
½ cup tomatoes, chopped
1 cup yellow bell pepper, chopped
⅔ cup cucumber, chopped
¼ cup green onions, chopped
3 tbsp tapenade (see note below)
2 tbsp lemon juice
¼ tsp black pepper

In the Kitchen

Cook the pasta, rinse, and allow to cool to at least room temperature.

In a large bowl, combined the cooked pasta and beans and mix well. Add the tomatoes, peppers, cucumber, tapenade, and lemon juice and mix well.

Store in a plastic container or plastic bag.

At Camp

Serve on its own or as an accompaniment.

Makes 2 servings.

Tapenade is a spread made chiefly with olives, capers, and anchovies. You can buy it prepared at better grocery stores, or make your own.

Dinner

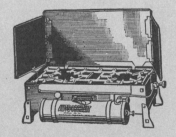

Dinner is usually the most elaborate meal of any wilderness trip. After a long day of hiking or other physical activity, a warm, hearty meal is just the thing to satisfy you. You can choose to incorporate different dishes as part of your dinner (e.g., salad, main, dessert), or have one large dish to share, preferably with protein and vegetables included.

Each of the dinner recipes makes two servings, so be advised if you are planning meals for larger parties. Know yourself and your eating habits; look over each recipe to see how they compare to the dinners you make at home. If you find yourself thinking, "I usually eat twice as much as this," you may want to adjust the recipes accordingly.

Note that recipes which have tofu as an ingredient should be prepared as the first night's meal, given the short shelf life of tofu.

Spinach & Tomato Rotini

2 cups fresh spinach, washed
½ cup sun-dried tomatoes, chopped
1 small onion, finely chopped
1 clove garlic, minced
½ tsp dried oregano
½ tsp dried basil
½ tsp salt
¼ tsp black pepper
1 tbsp olive oil
2 cups uncooked rotini pasta
½ cup Parmesan cheese, grated
4 cups water

In the Kitchen

Wash and dry the spinach and store in a plastic bag.

Combine the sun-dried tomatoes, onion, garlic, oregano, basil, salt, pepper, and oil and mix well. Store in a separate plastic bag.

Store the pasta and cheese in their own plastic bags.

At Camp

In a pot over high heat, boil the pasta for 10 minutes, rinse, and set aside.

In a separate pot over medium heat, sauté the tomato and onion mixture in oil until onions become tender. Add the spinach and cooked pasta, and continue to sauté until spinach becomes soft.

Sprinkle with Parmesan cheese.

Makes 2 servings.

Shrimp & Squash Penne

1 cup butternut squash, sliced thinly
1 cup zucchini, sliced thinly
2 cloves garlic, minced
1 tbsp olive oil
1 tbsp fresh lemon juice
½ tsp dried basil
½ tsp dried oregano
½ tsp salt
¼ tsp black pepper
2 cups uncooked penne pasta
¼ cup Parmesan cheese, grated
1 6-oz (170-g) can shrimp
4 cups water

In the Kitchen

In a bowl, combine the squash, zucchini, garlic, oil, lemon juice, basil, oregano, salt, and pepper and mix well. Store in a plastic bag.

Store the pasta and cheese in their own plastic bags.

At Camp

In a pot over high heat, boil the pasta for 10 minutes, rinse, and set aside.

In a large pot over medium heat, sauté the squash and zucchini until squash is tender. Add the shrimp and sauté for an additional minute. Add the cooked pasta and mix well. Sprinkle with Parmesan cheese.

Makes 2 servings.

Apricot Bulgur Pilaf

1½ cups bulgur
½ cup onion, chopped
½ cups dried apricots, chopped
2 tsp dried mint
2 tsp dried dill
3 tbsp dried parsley
2 tbsp olive oil
2 tbsp lemon juice
⅔ cup tomatoes, chopped
½ cup feta cheese
2¼ cups boiling water

In the Kitchen

Store the bulgur in a plastic bag.

In a bowl, combine the onions, apricots, mint, dill, parsley, oil and lemon juice and mix well. Store in a separate plastic bag.

Store the tomatoes and feta cheese together in a plastic bag.

At Camp

In a pot, boil the water and set aside.

In another pot over medium high heat, sauté the onions and apricots in oil until soft. Stir in the bulgur and sauté for another 2 minutes. Add the boiling water, cover, and bring to a boil again. Reduce heat and simmer gently for 10 minutes until bulgur is fluffy.

Add the tomatoes, then crumble the feta cheese over top and mix well.

Makes 2 servings.

Vegetable Tofu Stir-Fry

1 cup firm tofu, diced
2 cloves garlic, minced
½ cup onions, chopped
1 tbsp fresh ginger, grated
2 tbsp olive oil
3 tbsp soy sauce
1 cup broccoli, chopped into florets
½ cup celery, chopped large
½ cup carrots, chopped
½ cup red bell peppers, chopped
1 tsp sesame seeds (optional)

In the Kitchen

In a bowl, combine the tofu, garlic, onions, ginger, oil, and soy sauce and mix well. Store in a plastic bag.

Combine the broccoli, celery, carrots, red peppers, and sesame seeds and store in a plastic bag.

At Camp

In a large pot over medium heat, sauté the tofu and onions in oil, stirring continuously to ensure they do not burn. Once onions are soft and tofu starts to brown, add the vegetables. Continue stirring; add a tablespoon or so of water if mixture is getting dry. Once vegetables begin to soften, remove from heat.

Makes 2 servings.

To make this meal go further, or if you are preparing this for more than 2 people, serve over steamed rice.

Garlic Parmesan Vegetable Pasta

½ cup peas (fresh or frozen)
½ small onion, chopped
1 cup red bell peppers, chopped
1 cup yellow bell peppers, chopped
2 cloves garlic, minced
1 tbsp margarine or oil
¼ tsp salt
¼ tsp pepper
2 cups uncooked rotini pasta
½ cup Parmesan cheese, grated
4 cups water

In the Kitchen

In a bowl, combine the peas, onions, bell peppers, garlic, oil, salt, and pepper and mix well. Store in a plastic bag.

Store the pasta and cheese in their own plastic bags.

At Camp

In a pot over high heat, boil the pasta for 10 minutes, rinse, and set aside.

In a pot over medium high heat, sauté the vegetables in oil, stirring occasionally, until the vegetables are soft. Add the pasta and the Parmesan cheese and mix well.

Makes 2 servings.

FUN FACTS & TIPS!!!
Use baking soda instead of soap to wash off tree sap.

Shrimp & Feta Spaghetti

1¼ cup tomatoes, chopped
¼ cup green onions, chopped
¼ cup ripe black olives, sliced
1 clove garlic, minced
1 tsp dried dill
2 tsp olive oil
2 handfuls uncooked spaghetti
½ cup feta cheese
1 6-oz (170-g) can shrimp
4 cups water

In the Kitchen

In a bowl, combine the tomatoes, green onions, olives, garlic, dill, and oil and mix well. Store in a plastic bag.

Store the spaghetti in a plastic bag, breaking strands in half to fit if necessary.

Store the feta cheese in its own plastic bag.

Bring the can of shrimp.

At Camp

In a pot over high heat, boil the pasta for 10 minutes, rinse, and set aside.

In a pot over medium heat, sauté the shrimp and tomato mixture in oil for a few minutes until warmed through.

Add the pasta and feta cheese. Mix until cheese starts to melt.

Makes 2 servings.

Curried Veggie Bulgur

½ cup onions, chopped
1 tbsp olive oil
⅔ cup tomato, chopped
½ cup green bell peppers, chopped
½ cup carrots, chopped
½ tsp garlic powder
1 tbsp curry powder
1 tsp cumin
¼ tsp cayenne
¼ cup raisins
1½ cups bulgur
2½ cups water

In the Kitchen

Combine the onions and oil and store in a plastic bag.

Combine the tomatoes, green peppers, carrots, garlic powder, curry powder, cumin, cayenne, and raisins. Store in a plastic bag.

Store the bulgur in a plastic bag.

At Camp

In a pot, boil the water and set aside.

In another pot over medium heat, sauté the onions in oil until tender. Add the bulgur and sauté for another 2 minutes. Add the boiling water, cover, and bring to a boil again. Reduce heat and simmer gently until bulgur is fluffy.

Add the vegetables and cook for another 3 to 5 minutes, until carrots are soft.

Makes 2 servings.

Nutty Rice with Snow Peas & Peppers

¼ cup almond slices, toasted
1 cup snow peas, cut in half
½ cup red bell peppers, diced
½ cup yellow bell peppers, diced
½ cup onion, chopped
1 clove garlic, minced
1 tbsp olive oil
1 cup uncooked wild rice
2 cups water

In the Kitchen

Toast the almonds: Preheat oven to 325°F (160°C). Spread almonds on a dry baking sheet and toast for a couple of minutes until brown. When cool, store them in a plastic bag with the snow peas and peppers.

Combine the onions, garlic, and oil and store in a plastic bag.

Store the rice in a plastic bag.

At Camp

In a pot over medium high heat, sauté the onions and garlic in oil until onions are tender.

Add the rice and water. Bring to a boil, then reduce heat and let simmer until all the water has been absorbed.

Add the snow peas, peppers, and almonds and sauté until snow peas and peppers begin to soften.

Makes 2 servings.

Sweet Curried Couscous

1 cup couscous
1 tbsp olive oil
¼ cup green onions, chopped
½ cup red bell peppers, chopped
12 green beans, chopped
¼ cup raisins
5 dried dates or apricots, cut into chunks
2 tbsp curry powder
1 tsp paprika
1½ cups water

In the Kitchen

Store the couscous in a plastic bag.

In a bowl, combine the green onions, peppers, green beans, raisins, dates, curry powder, and paprika. Store in a plastic bag.

At Camp

In a pot, boil the water. Remove from heat and add the couscous and vegetables. Cover and let stand until all the liquid is absorbed.

Makes 2 servings.

Couscous is a Moroccan staple that makes an exotic alternative to rice or pasta.

Sausage & Zucchini Pasta

7 oz (200 g) cured Italian sausage
1½ cup zucchini, sliced
½ cup green bell peppers, chopped
⅓ cup fresh basil, chopped and packed down
1 tbsp olive oil
¼ tsp salt
¼ tsp pepper
2½ cups uncooked rotini pasta
¼ cup Parmesan cheese, grated
5 cups water

In the Kitchen

If possible, keep the sausage in its original packaging; this allows it to keep longer. Otherwise, chop it up and add to vegetables.

In a bowl, combine the zucchini, peppers, basil, oil, salt, and pepper and store in a plastic bag.

Store the pasta and cheese in their own plastic bags.

At Camp

In a pot of water over high heat, boil the pasta for 10 minutes. Drain and rinse.

Add the sausage and vegetables to pasta. Stir through until vegetables become soft and sausage is warmed through. Sprinkle with Parmesan cheese.

Makes 2 servings.

Penne with Green Beans & Sun-dried Tomatoes

½ cup sun-dried tomatoes

2 cups uncooked penne pasta

1½ cups green beans, chopped

2 cloves garlic, sliced

2 tbsp capers

2 tbsp olive oil

½ tsp salt

¼ tsp black pepper

¼ cup Romano or Parmesan cheese, grated

4 cups water

In the Kitchen

Wrap the sun-dried tomatoes in cellophane and store them with the pasta in a plastic bag.

In a bowl, combine the green beans, garlic, capers, oil, salt, and pepper and store in a plastic bag.

Store the cheese in a plastic bag.

At Camp

In a pot of water over high heat, boil the pasta for 10 minutes. Just before the pasta is done, add the tomatoes and continue cooking until tomatoes are soft. Drain, rinse, and set aside.

In another pot over medium high heat, sauté the green bean mixture in oil for 3 minutes, stirring occasionally.

Add the cooked pasta, tomatoes, and cheese. Stir until warmed through.

Makes 2 servings.

Ziti with Mushroom & Pepper Sauce

3 cups button mushrooms, sliced

½ cup green bell peppers, sliced thinly

2 cloves garlic, minced

¼ tsp dried rosemary

1 tbsp parsley

1 tbsp olive oil

¼ tsp salt

¼ tsp black pepper

¼ cup Parmesan cheese, grated

2 cups uncooked ziti pasta (or another tube pasta)

4 cups water

In the Kitchen

Combine the mushrooms, green peppers, garlic, rosemary, parsley, oil, salt, and pepper and store in a plastic bag.

Store the pasta and cheese in their own plastic bags.

At Camp

In a pot of water over high heat, boil the pasta for 10 minutes. Drain and rinse.

In another pot over medium heat, sauté the mushroom and pepper mixture in oil for 3 minutes or until the mushrooms are slightly tender.

Add the cooked pasta and mix together. Sprinkle with cheese.

Makes 2 servings.

FUN FACTS & TIPS!!!
To keep marshmallows from sticking together, add a tablespoon of powdered sugar.

Pine Nut & Peppers Penne

½ cup pine nuts, toasted
1 cup corn kernels
2 cups spinach, washed and trimmed
1 cup snow peas
½ cup green bell pepper, sliced
½ cup red bell pepper, sliced
¼ tsp salt
¼ tsp pepper
2 cups uncooked penne pasta
½ cup Parmesan cheese, grated
4 cups water

In the Kitchen

Toast the pine nuts: Preheat oven to 325°F (160°C). Spread pine nuts on a dry baking sheet and toast for a few minutes until brown.

Remove the kernels from a raw cob of corn with a knife. Combine the corn, toasted pine nuts, spinach, snow peas, bell peppers, salt, and pepper and store in a plastic bag.

Store the pasta and cheese and store in their own plastic bags.

At Camp

In a pot of water over high heat, boil the pasta for 10 minutes. Drain and rinse.

In a pot over medium high heat, sauté the vegetable and pine nut mixture until the peppers are soft.

Add pasta to vegetables and mix well. Sprinkle with cheese and mix well.

Makes 2 servings.

Cheesy Tomato Pasta

⅔ cup tomatoes, chopped
½ cup carrots, chopped
¾ cup Brie cheese, cubed
1 clove garlic, minced
3 tbsp fresh basil, finely chopped
1 tbsp olive oil
1 tsp red wine vinegar
¼ tsp fresh rosemary
¼ tsp dried rosemary
¼ tsp salt
¼ tsp ground black pepper
2 cups uncooked shell pasta
2 tsp Parmesan cheese, grated
4 cups water

In the Kitchen

In a large bowl, combine the tomatoes, carrots, Brie cheese, garlic, basil, oil, vinegar, rosemary, salt, and pepper and mix well. Store in a plastic container or bag (perhaps 2 of the latter to ensure there is no leakage).

Store the pasta and Parmesan cheese in their own plastic bags.

At Camp

In a pot of water over high heat, boil the pasta for 10 minutes. Drain and rinse.

Add the tomato mixture to pasta. Stir until the Brie melts and tomatoes become soft.

Sprinkle with Parmesan cheese.

Makes 2 servings.

Smoked Salmon & Asparagus Pasta

1½ cups asparagus, chopped into 1-inch pieces
2 cloves garlic, crushed
3 tbsp parsley, chopped
4 oz (100 g) smoked salmon, sliced
Package of dry Alfredo sauce
   (+ ingredients that it requires; usually butter + milk; see note below)
salt and pepper to taste
2 cups uncooked penne pasta
4 cups water

In the Kitchen

Combine the asparagus, garlic, and parsley and store in a plastic bag.

Wrap the salmon in cellophane and then store either in a plastic container or wrap with tin foil.

Gather and store the ingredients of the Alfredo sauce.

Store the pasta in a plastic bag.

At Camp

In a pot of water over high heat, boil the pasta for 10 minutes. Drain and rinse.

In a pot, prepare the Alfredo sauce according to the directions on the package.

Add the asparagus mixture and salmon and cook until sauce thickens.
Add the cooked pasta to sauce and mix well.

Makes 2 servings.

For milk, it may be easier and safer to bring milk powder which you can add water to.

Outdoor Wrapping

Wraps are a relatively new phenomenon that are perfect for portable eating; they're even easier to eat than sandwiches since all the ingredients are safely tucked inside the wrap. They can be filled them with all kinds of nutritious and tasty items. You can make your wraps either at home (and then pack for a trail lunch or cold dinner), or prepare them in the backcountry. If you are making the wraps at home, "wrap" them well in cellophane or tin foil.

Curry Wrap

½ cup onions, chopped
½ cup peas (fresh or frozen)
1 cup cauliflower, chopped
½ cup red bell pepper, chopped
½ cup green bell pepper, chopped
2 tsp fresh ginger, minced
2 tsp ground cumin
2 tsp mustard seeds
2 tsp ground coriander
2 tsp dried dill
1 tbsp olive oil
1 14-oz (396-ml) can lentils
4 flour wraps (choose from different flavors)

In the Kitchen

Combine the onions, peas, cauliflower, bell peppers, ginger, cumin, mustard seeds, coriander, dill, and oil and store in a plastic bag.

Either drain the lentils and store in a plastic bag or bring the can.

Store the wraps in cellophane or tin foil.

At Camp

In a pot over medium high heat, combine the vegetable mixture and lentils and cook until vegetables are soft; you may have to add up to ½ cup of water to help soften the cauliflower.

Divide mixture into 4 portions and spoon into wraps, then roll up.

Makes 4 wraps.

Consider bringing along some peanut sauce (page 120) to dip your wraps in.

Mexi-Bean Wrap

½ cup red onions, chopped
1 cup red bell peppers, chopped
1 cup green bell peppers, chopped
2 cloves garlic, minced
1 tsp chili powder
1 tsp ground cumin
1 tbsp olive oil
1 14-oz (396-ml) can black beans
½ cup cheddar cheese (preferably old), grated
½ cup cilantro, chopped
4 soft tortillas, wheat or corn

In the Kitchen

In a bowl, combine the onions, bell peppers, garlic, chili powder, cumin, and oil and store in a plastic bag.

Bring the can of black beans.

Store the cheddar cheese in a plastic bag.

Store the tortillas in cellophane or tin foil.

At Camp

In a pot, cook the black beans and vegetable mixture until vegetables are soft. Add a bit of water for extra moisture if necessary.

Divide mixture into 4 portions and spoon into tortillas, then roll up.

Makes 4 wraps.

Bulgur & Veggie Wraps

1½ cups bulgur
½ cup broccoli, chopped very small
¼ cup celery, chopped
½ cup snow peas, cut in half
½ cup onions, chopped
½ cup pumpkin seeds
1 tsp ground cumin
1 tsp dried dill
1 clove garlic, crushed
1 tsp mustard seeds
1 tsp black pepper
4 soft tortillas
2½ cups water

In the Kitchen

Store bulgur and place in a plastic bag.

Combine the broccoli, celery, snow peas, onions, pumpkin seeds, cumin, dill, garlic, mustard seeds, and pepper and store in a plastic bag.

Store the tortillas in cellophane or tin foil.

At Camp

In a pot, boil the water and set aside.

In a separate pot over medium heat, sauté the bulgur for 2 minutes and then add the hot water. Cover and bring to a boil again. Reduce heat and cook until all the water has evaporated and bulgur is fluffy.

Add the vegetable and spice mixture and mix well. Cook until vegetables are soft, about 15 minutes.

Divide mixture into 4 portions and spoon out into tortillas, then roll up.

Makes 4 wraps.

Smoked Salmon Wrap

3 oz (100 g) smoked salmon
¼ cup green onions, chopped
1 cup red bell peppers, sliced lengthwise
½ celery, chopped
2 tbsp fresh dill
¼ tsp salt
¼ tsp pepper
2 tbsp light Italian salad dressing
¾ cup uncooked wild rice
4 spinach wraps
1½ cups water

In the Kitchen

In a bowl, combine the salmon, onions, bell peppers, celery, dill, salt, pepper, and dressing and store in a plastic container or bag.

Store rice in a plastic bag.

Store the wraps in cellophane or tin foil.

At Camp

In a pot of water over high heat, bring the rice to a boil. Reduce heat to low and simmer until water is absorbed.

Add the salmon and vegetable mixture to the cooked rice. Mix until salmon and vegetables are warmed through.

Divide mixture into 4 portions and spoon into wraps, then roll up.

Makes 4 wraps.

Cheese & Vegetable-Stuffed Tortillas

½ cup onions, chopped
1 clove garlic, minced
1 cup green bell peppers, chopped
1 cup red bell peppers, chopped
⅔ cup broccoli, chopped
½ cup carrots, chopped
1 tbsp olive oil
¼ tsp black pepper
½ tsp chili powder
½ tsp dried parsley
⅔ cup cheddar cheese, shredded
4 soft tortillas

In the Kitchen

Store the onions and garlic in a plastic bag.

Combine the bell peppers, broccoli, carrots, oil, pepper, chili powder, and parsley and store in a plastic bag.

Store the grated cheese in a plastic bag.

Store the tortillas in cellophane or tin foil.

At Camp

In a pot over medium high heat, sauté the garlic and onions in oil, then add vegetable mixture and sauté until vegetables are soft.

Divide into 4 portions and spoon into tortillas. Add cheese on top and roll up.

To make this dish go further, cook a cup of rice to add to the vegetables.

Nutty-Fruity Rice

1 peach, chopped (about ⅔ cup)
½ cup red bell peppers, chopped
2 tbsp lime juice
pinch cayenne pepper
¼ tsp black pepper
½ cup nuts (cashews or almonds)
1 cup uncooked rice
2 cups water

In the Kitchen

In a bowl, combine the chopped peach, bell peppers, lime juice, cayenne, pepper, and nuts and store in a plastic bag.

Store the rice in a plastic bag.

At Camp

In a pot of water over high heat, cook the rice (bring to a boil, then simmer until water is absorbed).

Add rest of ingredients to cooked rice and mix well until they are warmed through.

Makes 2 servings.

Cranberry Rice Pilaf

½ cup celery, chopped
½ cup carrots, thinly sliced
¼ cup green onions, sliced
½ cup dried cranberries
2 tbsp orange zest, grated
juice of half an orange
½ tsp paprika
¼ tsp salt
¼ tsp black pepper
1 bouillon cube, chicken or vegetable
1 cup uncooked wild rice
2 cups water

In the Kitchen

In a bowl, combine the celery, carrots, green onions, cranberries, orange zest, orange juice, paprika, salt, and pepper and store in a plastic bag.

Bring the bouillon cube. Store the rice in a plastic bag.

At Camp

In a pot of water over high heat, cook the rice with the bouillon cube: bring to a boil, then simmer until half the water is absorbed.

Add the vegetable mixture and continue cooking until the water is fully absorbed and the rice is cooked. Mix well.

Makes 2 servings.

Presto! Shrimp-Pesto Pasta

Pesto Sauce:

3 large cloves garlic

¼ cup pine nuts, toasted

1½ cup fresh basil

¼ tsp salt

¼ tsp black pepper

¾ cup olive oil

½ cup Parmesan cheese, grated

Pasta:

1 cup pesto sauce

1 cup tomatoes, chopped

½ cup black olives, pits removed

¼ tsp salt

¼ tsp pepper

2 cups uncooked fusilli pasta

¼ cup Parmesan cheese, grated

1 6-oz (170-g) can shrimp packed
   in water

4 cups water

In the Kitchen

For the pesto sauce: Toast the pine nuts: Preheat oven to 325°F (160°C). Spread pine nuts on a dry baking sheet and toast for a few minutes until brown.

In a blender or food processor, purée the garlic, pine nuts, bail, salt, and pepper. Slowly add the oil while puréeing. Once mixed, stir in the Parmesan cheese.

Combine the pesto sauce, tomatoes, olives, salt, and pepper and store in a plastic bag.

Store the pasta and cheese (for pasta) in separate plastic bags.

Bring the can of shrimp.

At Camp

In a pot of water over high heat, boil the pasta for 10 minutes. Drain and rinse.

Add the shrimp, pesto sauce, tomatoes, and olives. Mix well and cook until heated through. Sprinkle with Parmesan cheese, and season with salt and pepper.

Makes 2 servings.

FUN FACTS & TIPS!!!
Bring extra plastic bags; you will always find use for them, whether it's garbage, wrapping leftovers, or storing wet dishes.

Tuna-Veggie Couscous

1 cob of corn, kernels removed
½ cup carrots, chopped
½ green bell peppers, chopped
¼ cup red onions, chopped
1 garlic clove, crushed
1 tsp ground cumin
1 tsp fresh dill, chopped
1 tbsp olive oil
¾ cup feta cheese
1 cup couscous
1 6-oz (170-g) can tuna in water
1½ cups of water

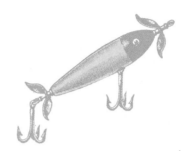

In the Kitchen

In a bowl, combine the corn, carrots, bell peppers, red onions, cumin, dill, and oil and store in a plastic bag.

Store the cheese and couscous in their own plastic bags.

Bring the can of tuna.

At Camp

In a pot over medium high heat, sauté the vegetables in oil until onions are tender. Add the tuna. Remove from heat.

In a second pot, boil the water. Add the couscous to the vegetable mixture and add in the water. Cover and allow water to be absorbed.

Add the cheese and mix well.

Mac & Cheese

I've had my share of macaroni and cheese disasters, but this is about moving past my pain to mac and cheese enlightenment!

The easiest way to prepare mac and cheese in the backcountry is to use the boxed versions which require margarine and milk (although I suggest you use water instead to avoid the dangers of spoiled milk). Sure, it's not quite the same as home-made mac and cheese, but it fills the void, especially with the variations that follow here.

Use whatever brand of mac and cheese you prefer. Keep in mind, though, that these recipes are designed to be used with regular mac and cheese; if you want to use other flavors, go right ahead!

Cooking M&C the Easy Way

- Empty the box of pasta into a plastic bag. Store the margarine in a film canister, and bring along the packet of cheese as is.

- After your pasta is cooked, drain the water except for a little bit, which takes the place of milk. Add the margarine and the cheese, then use one of the following recipes to fancy it up. Enjoy!

M&C: Variations on a Theme

These recipes are to be used once your packaged macaroni and cheese has been cooked.

Touch o' Tuna

¼ cup green onions, chopped
½ cup tomatoes, chopped
2 tsp Spike seasoning salt
1 6-oz (170-g) can of tuna in water

In the Kitchen

Combine the green onions, tomatoes, and seasoning salt and store in a plastic bag.

Bring the can of tuna.

At Camp

Once pasta is cooked and drained (except for a bit of water), add the margarine, cheese, vegetable mixture, and tuna. Mix well and continue to cook until warmed through.

Makes 2 servings.

Basic Broccoli

1 cup broccoli, chopped into florets

In the Kitchen

Store the broccoli in a plastic bag.

At Camp

When pasta is almost finished cooking, add the broccoli in the water and continue cooking until tender. Drain (except for a bit of water), then add margarine and cheese. Mix well.

Makes 2 servings.

Tex-Mex

½ cup green bell peppers, chopped
1 14-oz (396-ml) can kidney beans
½ package taco seasoning

In the Kitchen

Store the green peppers in a plastic bag.

Bring the can of the beans.

At Camp

Drain the can of beans.

Once pasta is cooked and drained (except for a bit of water), add the margarine, cheese, taco seasoning, beans, and green peppers. Mix well and continue to cook until warmed through.

Makes 2 servings.

The Veg-Out

½ cup peas (fresh or frozen)
¼ cup green onions, chopped
½ cup red bell peppers, chopped
½ cup carrots, chopped

In the Kitchen

Store all the vegetables in a plastic bag.

At Camp

Once pasta is cooked and drained (except for a bit of water), add the vegetables, cheese, and margarine. Mix well.

Makes 2 servings.

The Mighty Greek

½ cup feta cheese

½ cup tomatoes, chopped

½ cup green bell peppers, chopped

¼ cup red onions, chopped

¼ cup black olives, pits removed

¼ tsp fresh mint

¼ tsp dried dill

¼ tsp dried oregano

In the Kitchen

Store the cheese in a plastic bag.

Combine the rest of the ingredients and store in a plastic bag.

At Camp

Once pasta is cooked and drained (except for a bit of water), add the vegetable mixture and continue to cook until vegetables soften. Crumble the cheese and add along with the margarine. Mix well.

Makes 2 servings.

Risotto Without the Pain-O

½ cup sun-dried tomatoes, chopped
1 clove garlic, minced
2 tbsp fresh basil, chopped
1 tsp dried dill
1 cup uncooked rice (see note below)
¾ cup Parmesan cheese, grated
2 cups water

In the Kitchen

Combine the sun-dried tomatoes, garlic, basil, and dill in a plastic bag.

Store the rice and cheese in their own plastic bags.

At Camp

In a pot of water over high heat, bring the rice to a boil. Reduce heat to low and simmer until half the water is absorbed.

Add the vegetables and continue cooking until all the water is absorbed.

Add the cheese and mix well until cheese is melted.

Makes 2 servings.

This and the recipe that follows are not your traditional risottos, which are made with Arborio rice, but they taste just as great!

Rosemary Mushroom Risotto

1 cup button mushrooms, sliced
1 tbsp dried rosemary
¼ tsp ground cumin
1 clove garlic, minced
1 cup uncooked rice
¾ cup Parmesan cheese, grated
2 cups water

In the Kitchen

Combine the mushrooms, rosemary, cumin, and garlic in a plastic bag.

Store the rice and cheese in their own plastic bags.

At Camp

In a pot of water over high heat, bring the rice to a boil. Reduce heat to low and simmer until half the water is absorbed.

Add the mushroom mixture and continue cooking until all the water is absorbed.

Add the cheese and mix well until cheese is melted.

Makes 2 servings.

FUN FACTS & TIPS!!!
Cover your pots when cooking. Not only will they retain heat and cook faster, they'll also keep the bugs out.

Shrimp Jambalaya

1 cup tomatoes, chopped
¼ cup onions, chopped
½ cup green bell peppers, chopped
½ cup celery, chopped
½ tsp dried thyme
¼ tsp chili powder
¼ tsp cayenne pepper
¼ tsp paprika
1 bay leaf
1 6-oz (170-g) can shrimp
½ cup uncooked rice
1 vegetable or chicken bouillon cube
1½ cups water

In the Kitchen

Combine the vegetables and spices and store in a plastic bag.

Bring the can of shrimp.

Store the rice in a plastic bag. Bring the bouillon cube.

At Camp

In a pot of water over high heat, bring the rice to a boil.

Reduce heat and simmer until water is absorbed.

Keep rice on heat and add another ½ cup of water.

Add the vegetable mixture and shrimp and mix well. Cook until vegetables are tender.

Makes 2 servings.

Spinach Feta Rice

3 cups spinach, washed
½ cup onions, chopped
2 cloves garlic, minced
1 tsp dried dill
1 tsp dried oregano
½ tsp dried basil
½ tsp nutmeg
½ tsp black pepper
½ cup feta cheese
1 cup uncooked rice
1 chicken or vegetable bouillon cube
2 cups water
salt and pepper to taste

In the Kitchen

Combine the spinach, onions, garlic, dill, oregano, basil, nutmeg, and pepper and store in a plastic bag.

Store the cheese and rice in their own plastic bags. Bring the bouillon cube.

At Camp

In a pot of water over high heat, bring the rice and bouillon cube to a boil. Reduce heat and simmer until ¾ of water is absorbed.

Add the spinach mixture and cook until all the water is absorbed.

Add the cheese. Mix well and continue cooking until slightly melted.

Add salt and pepper to taste.

Makes 2 servings.

Cauliflower & Potato Curry

1½ cups cauliflower, chopped into florets
¼ cup onions, chopped
⅔ cup tomatoes, chopped
1 cup peas (fresh or frozen)
1 tsp curry powder
1 tsp ground cumin
1 tsp mustard seed
½ tsp salt
½ tsp black pepper
2 medium potatoes (any kind)
1 vegetable or chicken bouillon cube
2 cups water

In the Kitchen

Combine the cauliflower, onions, tomatoes, peas, and spices and store in a plastic bag.

Keep the potatoes whole to chop At Camp. Bring the bouillon cube.

At Camp

Cut the potatoes into small chunks.

In a pot of water over high heat, combine all the ingredients and bring to a boil.

Continue cooking until potatoes are soft and mixture has reduced to a stew.

Makes 2 servings.

Serve with pita bread, and yogurt to cut the heat.

Festive Garden Soup

1 cup broccoli, chopped into florets
1 cup celery, chopped
½ cup carrots, chopped
¼ cup onions, chopped
1 cob of corn, kernels removed
2 cloves garlic, crushed
1 bay leaf
1 tsp dried basil
1 tsp dried oregano
¼ cup couscous
1 small white potato
1 chicken or vegetable bouillon cube
4 cups water

In the Kitchen

Combine the vegetables, garlic, and spices and store in a plastic bag.

Store the couscous in a plastic bag.

Bring the potato whole to chop At Camp. Bring the bouillon cube.

At Camp

Cut up the potato into small chunks.

In a large pot of water over high heat, combine the vegetables, potatoes, couscous and bouillon cube.

Bring to a boil and then simmer until potatoes are soft, about 10 minutes.

Makes 2 servings.

Serve with some pita or pumpernickel bread.

Caribbean Black Bean Soup

½ cup onions, chopped
½ cup carrots, chopped
½ cup celery, chopped
2 cloves garlic, minced
1 cup red bell peppers, chopped
1 cup green bell peppers, chopped
1 tbsp olive oil
2 tsp ground cumin
½ tsp black pepper
1 tsp allspice
1 19-oz (538-ml) can black beans
3 cups water

In the Kitchen

In a bowl, combine the onions, carrots, celery, bell peppers, oil, cumin, pepper, and allspice and store in a plastic bag.

Bring the can of beans.

At Camp

In a pot over medium high heat, sauté the vegetable mixture in oil until onions and carrots begin to soften.

Add the black beans and water. Mix well, increase heat, and bring to a boil.

Reduce heat to low and simmer for 10 minutes.

Makes 2 servings.

Garnish this dish with salsa or cilantro. This goes well with My Mom's Cornbread (page 57).

Minestrone Soup

¾ cup onions, chopped
½ cup carrots, chopped
½ cup celery, chopped
2 tbsp parsley, chopped
2 tbsp fresh basil, chopped
2 tbsp olive oil
1 19-oz (538-ml) can diced tomatoes (see note below)
1 vegetable or chicken bouillon cube
⅔ cup uncooked small shell pasta
2½ cups water

In the Kitchen

In a bowl, combine the onions, carrots, celery, parsley, basil, and oil and store in a plastic bag.

Keep the tomatoes in the can. Bring the bouillon cube.

Store the pasta in its own plastic bag.

At Camp

In a pot over medium high heat, sauté the vegetable mixture until the onions are soft.

Add the tomatoes, pasta, bouillon cube, and water. Mix well, increase heat, and bring to a boil.

Reduce heat and simmer for 10 minutes.

Makes 2 servings.

Some canned diced tomatoes are available "spiced"; use these for a bit of extra kick.

Tomato & Lentil Soup

⅔ cup tomatoes, chopped
1 cup cauliflower, chopped
½ cup onions, chopped
1 clove garlic, minced
1 tsp ground cumin
½ tsp salt
½ tsp nutmeg
1 tbsp olive oil
½ cup dried red lentils
1 vegetable bouillon cube
3 cups water

In the Kitchen

In a bowl, combine the tomatoes, cauliflower, onions, garlic, cumin, salt, nutmeg, and oil and store in a plastic bag.

Store the lentils in a plastic bag. Bring the bouillon cube.

At Camp

In a pot over medium high heat, sauté the vegetable mixture in oil until onions begin to soften.

Add the lentils, bouillon cube, and water.

Bring to a boil, then reduce heat to low and simmer until lentils are soft.

Makes 2 servings.

FUN FACTS & TIPS!!!
Stretching: always a good idea! Cramps during your hike are not a fun thing.

Cheesy Broccoli & Cauliflower

1½ cups broccoli, chopped
1½ cups cauliflower, chopped
¾ cup Parmesan cheese, grated
2 tbsp butter
salt and pepper to taste

In the Kitchen

Store the broccoli and califlower in a plastic bag.

Store the cheese in a plastic bag and the butter in a film canister.

At Camp

In a pot of water over high heat, boil the broccoli and cauliflower for about 5 minutes until they are just soft. Drain.

Add the cheese and butter and mix well. Season with salt and pepper.

Makes 2 servings.

This makes a great accompaniment to a main dish.

Avocado & Asparagus Pasta

1 firm avocado
1½ cups asparagus, chopped (about 12 stalks)
¼ cup red onions, minced
2 tbsp olive oil
2 tbsp lemon juice
½ tsp red pepper flakes
¼ tsp salt
¼ tsp black pepper
2 cups uncooked shell pasta
¼ cup Parmesan cheese, grated
4 cups water

In the Kitchen

Store the whole avocado in a plastic bag.

In a bowl, the asparagus, red onions, oil, lemon juice, red pepper flakes, salt, and pepper and store in a plastic bag.

Store the pasta and cheese in their own plastic bags.

At Camp

In a pot of water over high heat, boil the pasta for 10 minutes. Drain and rinse.

Chop up the avocado into large chunks and combine with the asparagus mixture.

Add mixture to pasta and reduce heat to medium. Mix well until the asparagus is soft.

Sprinkle with Parmesan cheese.

Makes 2 servings.

Vegetable Paella

¼ cups red onions, chopped
1 cup tomatoes, chopped
¾ cup yellow bell peppers, chopped
¾ cup peas (fresh or frozen)
2 cloves garlic, minced
½ cup cashew nuts
1 tsp dried thyme
¼ tsp saffron
pinch cayenne pepper
1 tbsp olive oil
1 vegetable or chicken bouillon cube
1 cup uncooked brown rice
2 cups water

In the Kitchen

In a bowl, combine the red onions, tomatoes, bell peppers, peas, garlic, cashews, thyme, saffron, cayenne, and oil and store in a plastic bag.

Store the rice in a plastic bag. Bring the bouillon cube.

At Camp

In a pot of water over high heat, bring the rice and bouillon cube to a boil. Reduce heat to low.

When half of the water has been absorbed, add the vegetable mixture and mix well.

Continue to simmer until all the water is absorbed.

Makes 2 servings.

Saffron is the most expensive spice in the world, but used sparingly it makes a world of difference to dishes and is essential for paella!

Good Ol' Fashioned Beans & Rice

1 cup tomatoes, chopped
1 cup green bell peppers, chopped
½ cup onions, chopped
1 clove garlic, minced
½ tsp celery seed
1 tsp ground cumin
½ tsp chilli powder
¼ tsp cayenne pepper
½ tsp salt
¼ tsp black pepper
1 tsp Worcestershire sauce
1 tsp oil
1 cup uncooked rice
¼ cup cheddar cheese, grated
¼ cup cilantro, chopped
1 14-oz (396-ml) can kidney beans
2 cups water

In the Kitchen

In a bowl, combine the tomatoes, bell peppers, onions, garlic, celery seed, cumin, chili powder, cayenne, salt, pepper, Worcestershire sauce, salt, and pepper and store in a plastic bag.

Store the rice in a plastic bag.

Store the cheese and cilantro in a plastic bag.

Bring the can of beans.

At Camp

In a pot of water, bring the rice to a boil. Reduce heat to low.

When half of the water has been absorbed, add the vegetable mixture and beans (drained) and mix well.

Continue to cook until all the water has been absorbed.

Garnish with cheese and cilantro.

Makes 2 servings.

Ginger Vegetable Rice

¾ cup carrots, sliced

¾ cup celery, sliced

1 cup green bell peppers, chopped

½ cup onions, chopped

2 tbsp fresh ginger, grated

2 cloves garlic, minced

½ cup cashew nuts

⅛ tsp cayenne pepper

¼ tsp salt

¼ tsp pepper

1 tbsp sesame oil

1 cup uncooked rice

2 cups water

In the Kitchen

In a bowl, combine the carrots, celery, bell peppers, onions, ginger, garlic, cashews, cayenne, salt, pepper, and oil and store in a plastic bag.

Store the rice in a plastic bag.

At Camp

In a pot of water over high heat, bring the rice to a boil. Reduce to low and simmer until water is absorbed.

In another pot over medium high heat, sauté the vegetable mixture until the carrots are just soft; add a tablespoon of water if necessary.

Add the cooked rice and mix well.

Makes 2 servings.

Pineapple Fried Rice

1 cup medium firm tofu, cut into chunks
½ cup peas (fresh or frozen)
2 cloves garlic, minced
pinch cayenne pepper
2 tbsp olive oil
1 cup uncooked rice
1 14-oz (396-ml) can pineapple chunks
2 cups water

In the Kitchen

In a bowl, combine the tofu, peas, garlic, cayenne, and oil and store in a plastic bag.

Store the rice in a plastic bag.

Bring the can of pineapple chunks.

At Camp

In a pot of water, bring the rice to a boil. Reduce heat to low and simmer until all the water is absorbed.

In another pot over medium high heat, combine the tofu mixture and pineapple and sauté until everything is warmed through.

Add the cooked rice and mix well.

Makes 2 servings.

FUN FACTS & TIPS!!!
Laundry lint from your pockets makes for a good fire starter.

Rice With Roasted Corn & Pine Nuts

⅓ cup pine nuts, toasted
1 cob of corn, kernels removed, toasted
½ cup zucchini, chopped
½ cup green bell peppers, chopped
½ cup red onions, chopped
¼ tsp salt
¼ tsp pepper
1 cup uncooked rice
¼ cup Parmesan cheese, grated
2 cups water

In the Kitchen

Preheat oven to 325°F (160°C). Spread pine nuts and corn kernels on a dry baking sheet and bake for about 10 minutes until nuts are brown, stirring occasionally to ensure they don't burn. Let cool. Combine in a plastic bag.

In a bowl, combine the zucchini, bell peppers, red onions, salt, and pepper and store in a plastic bag.

Store the rice and cheese in their own plastic bags.

At Camp

In a pot of water over high heat, bring the rice to a boil. Reduce heat to low and simmer. When half of the water has been absorbed, add the zucchini mixture and mix well.

Continue to cook until all the water is absorbed.

Add the pine nuts and corn. Mix well and cook for an additional 2 minutes.

Sprinkle with Parmesan cheese.

Makes 2 servings.

Nutty Artichoke Couscous

½ cup walnuts, toasted
3 marinated artichoke hearts (from a jar), cut into quarters
½ cup red bell peppers, chopped
½ cup onions, chopped
½ tsp nutmeg
1 tsp mint
1 tsp dried dill
½ cup feta cheese
1 cup couscous
1½ cups water

In the Kitchen

Toast the walnuts: Turn oven to broil. Spread walnuts on a dry cookie sheet and toast for a few minutes until brown, stirring occasionally to ensure they don't burn. Let cool.

In a bowl, combine the walnuts, artichoke hearts, red peppers, onions, nutmeg, mint, and dill and store in a plastic bag.

Store the cheese and coucous in their own plastic bags.

At Camp

Bring a pot of water over high heat to a boil. Add the couscous, reduce heat to low and simmer until all the water is absorbed.

In another pot over medium high heat, sauté the walnut and artichoke mixture in oil until the onions are soft. Add the couscous and mix well.

Crumble in the feta cheese and mix well until it starts to melt.

Makes 2 servings.

Hearty Veggie Chili

1½ cup tomatoes, chopped
½ cup green bell peppers, chopped
½ cup onions, chopped
1 cob of corn, kernels removed
2 cloves garlic, minced
1 tbsp chili powder
½ tsp dried oregano
½ tsp sugar
½ tsp salt
½ tsp black pepper
1 14-oz (396-ml) can kidney beans
¼ cup cheddar cheese, grated
¼ cup cilantro, chopped
½ cup water

In the Kitchen

In a bowl, combine the tomatoes, bell peppers, onions, corn, garlic, chili powder, oregano, sugar, salt, and pepper and store in a plastic bag.

Keep the beans in the can.

Store the cheese and cilantro in a plastic bag.

At Camp

In a pot over medium heat, combine the vegetable mixture, beans, and water and bring to a boil, stirring often to ensure it doesn't burn. Reduce heat to low and simmer for 10-15 minutes.

Garnish with cheese and cilantro.

Makes 2 servings.

Mop up this chili with My Mom's Cornbread (page 57).

Tofu Broccoli in Peanut Sauce

Peanut sauce:
¼ cup all-natural peanut butter
2 cloves garlic, minced
1 tbsp fresh ginger, minced
2 tbsp honey
1 tbsp lime juice
1 tbsp sesame oil
2 tbsp soy sauce
2 tbsp rice wine vinegar
3 tbsp coconut milk

In the Kitchen

For the peanut sauce: in a blender or food processor, purée all the ingredients until smooth. Store in a plastic container or bag (bring more than you need, in case of spillage).

In a bowl, combine the tofu, broccoli, onions, carrots, and oil and store in a plastic bag.

Tofu Broccoli:
2 cup firm tofu, chopped
2½ cups broccoli, chopped
¼ cup onions, chopped
½ cup carrots, chopped
1 tbsp olive oil
1 cup peanut sauce

At Camp

In a pot over medium high heat, sauté the tofu and broccoli mixture until the vegetables are just soft; add a tablespoon of water if necessary.

Add the peanut sauce and mix well until warmed through.

Makes 2 servings.

Eggplant and Tomato Bow-Ties

1½ cup eggplant, chopped
½ cup green bell peppers, chopped
½ cup onions, chopped
1 clove garlic, minced
2 tsp dried oregano
1 tsp dried basil
½ tsp salt
2 tbsp olive oil
1 19-oz (538-ml) can diced tomatoes
2 cups uncooked farfelle pasta (bow-ties)
4 cups water

In the Kitchen

In a bowl, combine the eggplant, bell peppers, onions, garlic, oregano, basil, salt, and oil and store in a plastic bag.

Bring the can of tomatoes. Store the pasta in a plastic bag.

At Camp

In a pot of water over high heat, boil the pasta for 10 minutes. Drain and rinse.

In another pot over medium high heat, sauté the eggplant mixture and tomatoes until the eggplant is soft.

Add the pasta and mix well.

Makes 2 servings.

Shrimp Primavera

1 cup red bell peppers, chopped
1 cup green bell peppers, chopped
⅔ cup tomatoes, chopped
½ cup onion, chopped
2 cloves garlic, minced
1 tsp dried oregano
½ tsp black pepper
1 tsp olive oil
1 6-oz (170-g) can shrimp
2 cups uncooked penne pasta
4 cups water

In the Kitchen

In a bowl, combine the bell peppers, tomatoes, onions, garlic, oregano, pepper, and oil and store in a plastic bag.

Bring the can of shrimp. Store the pasta in a plastic bag.

At Camp

In a pot of water over high heat, boil the pasta for 10 minutes. Drain and rinse.

In another pot over medium high heat, sauté the pepper and tomato mixture until onions are soft.

Add the pasta and shrimp and mix well until warmed through.

Makes 2 servings.

FUN FACTS & TIPS!!!
Waterproof matches by dipping the heads in nail polish.

Spicy Thai Shrimp

1 cup broccoli, chopped into florets
½ cup yellow bell peppers, chopped
1 cup celery, chopped
1 cup carrots, chopped
1 tbsp fresh ginger, minced
½ tsp red pepper flakes
2 tbsp fresh cilantro, chopped
2 tbsp hoisin sauce
1 tbsp fish sauce
1 tbsp lime juice
2 tbsp honey
1 tbsp rice wine vinegar
2 tsp sesame oil
1 6-oz (170-g) can shrimp

 In the Kitchen

In a bowl, combine all the ingredients except the shrimp and mix well. Store in a plastic bag.

Bring the can of shrimp.

 At Camp

In a pot over medium high heat, sauté the vegetable mixture and shrimp until vegetables are tender.

Makes 2 servings.

 *Hoisin sauce and fish sauce can be found in Asian markets and better grocery stores. This dish can be served as is or, for a heartier meal or more people, over rice.*

Penne Lasagna

1½ cups tomatoes, chopped
1 cup mushrooms, sliced
1 cup spinach, washed
1 tbsp dried oregano
¼ tsp nutmeg
¼ tsp salt
¼ tsp pepper
2 cups uncooked penne pasta
½ cup ricotta cheese
4 cups water

In the Kitchen

In a bowl, combine the tomatoes, mushrooms, spinach, oregano, nutmeg, salt, and pepper and store in a plastic bag.

Store the pasta and cheese in their own plastic bags.

At Camp

In a pot of water over high heat, boil the pasta for 10 minutes. Drain and rinse.

Add the vegetable mixture and mix over medium heat until the tomatoes are just soft.

Add the ricotta cheese and mix well until melted through.

Makes 2 servings.

Dal Lentils

½ cup green bell peppers, chopped
½ cup peas (fresh or frozen)
½ cup onions, chopped
1 clove garlic, minced
1 tbsp fresh ginger, minced
1 tbsp olive oil
2 tbsp curry powder
1 tsp ground cumin
½ tsp salt
½ tsp pepper
½ cup uncooked brown rice
1 16-oz (453-ml) can lentils
2 cups water

In the Kitchen

In a bowl, combine the bell peppers, peas, onions, garlic, ginger, and oil and store in a plastic bag.

Combine the curry, cumin, salt, and pepper and store in a film canister.

Store the rice in a plastic bag. Bring the can of lentils.

At Camp

In a pot of water over high heat, bring the rice to a boil. Reduce heat to low and simmer until water has been absorbed.

In another pot over medium high heat, sauté the vegetable mixture for a few minutes until onions are just soft. Add the spices and lentils (drained) and mix well. Continue to cook for 10 minutes.

Serve over rice.

Makes 2 servings.

Fried Rice with Shrimp

1 cup green cabbage, chopped
½ cup celery, chopped
1 green onion, chopped
2 cloves garlic, minced
1 tbsp fresh ginger, minced
1 tsp sesame oil
⅓ cup soy sauce
1 cup uncooked brown rice
1 6-oz (170-g) can shrimp
2 cups water

In the Kitchen

In a bowl, combine the cabbage, celery, green onion, garlic, ginger, oil, and soy sauce and store in a plastic bag.

Store the rice in a plastic bag. Bring the can of shrimp.

At Camp

In a pot of water over high heat, bring the rice to a boil. Reduce heat to low and simmer until all the water has been absorbed.

In another pot over medium high heat, sauté the vegetable mixture and shrimp until the cabbage is soft. Add to the rice and mix well.

Makes 2 servings.

Honey Balsamic Tomato Couscous

1 cup cherry tomatoes, cut in half
¾ cup cucumbers, diced
1 tbsp honey
2 tbsp balsamic vinegar
1 tsp dried basil
1 tbsp olive oil
1 cup couscous
1½ cups water

In the Kitchen

In a bowl, combine the tomatoes, cucumbers, honey, vinegar, basil, and oil and store in a plastic bag.

Store the couscous in a plastic bag.

At Camp

In a pot over high heat, bring the water to a boil. Remove from heat and add the couscous. Let stand until all the water has been absorbed.

Add the tomato mixture and mix well until warmed through.

Makes 2 servings.

Arugula Pasta

3 cups arugula, torn into pieces
½ cup red onions, diced
½ tsp black pepper
2 tbsp olive oil
1 cup gorgonzola cheese
2 cups uncooked rotini pasta
4 cups water

In the Kitchen

In a bowl, combine the arugula, red onions, pepper, and oil and store in a plastic bag.

Store the cheese and pasta in their own plastic bags.

At Camp

In a pot of water over high heat, boil the pasta for 10 minutes. Drain and rinse.

In another pot over medium high heat, sauté the vegetable mixture until the onions and arugula are just soft.

Add the pasta and cheese and mix well until cheese has melted.

Makes 2 servings.

Mixed Herb Pasta

1 cup mixed fresh herbs, chopped (e.g., basil, mint, parsley, sage)
⅔ cup red bell peppers, chopped
⅔ cup yellow bell peppers, chopped
¼ cup green onions, chopped
2 tbsp olive oil
¼ tsp salt
¼ tsp black pepper
¼ cup goat's cheese
2 cups uncooked fusilli pasta
4 cups water

In the Kitchen

Combine the herbs, bell peppers, green onions, oil, salt, and pepper and store in a plastic bag.

Store the cheese and pasta in their own plastic bags.

At Camp

In a pot of water over high heat, boil the pasta for 10 minutes. Drain and rinse.

In another pot over medium heat, sauté the vegetable mixture until the bell peppers are just soft. Add to the pasta.

Crumble the goat's cheese over top.

Makes 2 servings.

FUN FACTS & TIPS!!!
One-pot meals are the easiest in the winter. This will make sure that what you are consuming stays warm because once you stop moving, this is your source of heat.

Index

Index

Index

Index

Index

Index

Index

Index

Index

Index

Index

Index